To Artie
Happy 70th
Happy DAY!

Mike

DON'T FALL OFF THE MOUNTAIN

COLLECTED POEMS
1968-1998
MIKE PARKER

D'Spare Press
Boulder, Colorado

Don't Fall Off The Mountain
Collected Poems 1968 - 1998
© copyright 1998 by Mike Parker

D'Spare Press books are edited by Phil Dubitsky
2960 Lorraine Court - Boulder, Co. 80304
and can be ordered:
c/o D'Spare Press P.O. Box 256 Ward, Co. 80481

ACKNOWLEDGMENTS
The publishers would like to thank the editors of the follow-
ing periodicals where some of these poems first appeared:
*Magazine, Changes, The Noiseless Spider, Fried Shoes,
Bombay Gin, Glass House Gazette, Melt & Flood News,
Ward Sentinal Forum, Jail Bait, Underciti* -
Beggars Banquet Records Ltd., London, England -
"Whose Mama, Black & Broke, Tough Shit, Domestic Ser-
vants, Waterball Satellite, European Ashes, Alphabet Town
Special thanks to The Ward Factor
Photo credits: cover; Mike Parker & Phil Dubitsky
page 2-   Yukon River by John Mage
page 25-   Firehouse Crew by Steve LaRue
page 37-   Deputy, Magistrate & Marshal by Linda Wolf
page 112- KPFA studio 1978 - Carol LaMela, Mike Parker,
           Phil Dubitsky & Pat Marrocco by Leah Robinson
page 127- Ballistic Kisses Band: Mike Parker, Rich McClusky,
           Jeff Freund, Mike Hyrynk by Larry Toth
page 157- Damita & Mike by Leah Robinson
page 176- Drawing by Tall Bob Murray
page 208- about the author photo by Celeste Marrocco
Back cover - Nunchuck man by Larry Toth
Back cover photo live at Penny Lane by Idiot
IBSN: 0-9669180-0-2 *Library of Congress cataloging - publication data*

For Annie
& Phil
and for all my friends

This book is made possible by grants from
A.H.A.B. / Neodata Literary Fellowship
The W'E Foundation
and especially the Ward Public Library Artist In Residency
Program

CONTENTS

Peak T'Peak Poems 1968-1979

INTRODUCTION

Hanging around the millennium
waiting for the new age curtain to be drawn
he likes to watch the chorus girls
adjust their foundation in the wings
he writes graffiti on the censored signs

Thirty years of poetry, thirty years of Michael Parker's
poetry, that is this book. Some of us have been waiting a
long time for this, some of us dying for this, some of the
people in the earlier poems are not alive to read the latter
poems. People from the meanest streets in america to what
Gertrude Stein calls the "daily daily" of rural community
life, are captured here in a language and voice that makes
the english language bend. Bend to the journalistic need to
present what is right in front of us, but no one seems to be
seeing. Poetic graphics

Michael delivers his poetry like a bricklayer but the feeling
is more like a loving slap on a bare baby bottom. And just
when you are braced for a blast of blaring headlines he'll
drop a hot haiku in your lap.
I would say I have found two constants in these thirty years
of poetry, one they all come from the battle ground of the
class wars, and two, even the most inanimate object can
exude sexuality. I would suggest you take this book and
follow Michael's advice
don't fall off the mountain
sit &
climb

December 1, 1998
Greg Tebrich from the Longmont Hilton

nightbloom

bareass moon
drops drawers
on the ridge

snow capped
bridge stones
i walked thru
the water instead

the sandy
spring floor
didn't even spl . .
splash-

wrap my legs
around an ash
close my eyes
sigh - the white
nipple drips
milky

the wind
presses me
into you

snowing since yesterday
half a mountain showing
the pond a false clearing
& the road clear of old ruts

the evidence of life
a broken mound where fawn
got hung in the plow's drift

no one comes
so the plow liberates nothing
just making noise & muddy shoulders

spent the day
taking out
the standing
thin dead pine

here & there
snow patches
& new green moss
nests of deer leavings
still pellets
till berries come
& make it softer

the april ground
wet &
decidedly brown

all sap up
birch peel
& buds on
the high scrub
deer couldn't reach

sounds different
birds & the melting
creek all emotional
& loud
with yesterday's rain

old bulbs quietly
push through mulch
while wind
shatters the overcast

a truck full of empties
rattles over the bridge
it's the propane
guy & his kid

to myself stoned I
think it's a gas
going down the path
to bum a smoke
& shoot the shit

rock sweat
drips into fire
puffs steam
mad clouds
chilly Catskills
thai stick
mu tea
favorite cave

our own veils
tattered ripe
with wind

sit &
climb

.

Today I saw a murder take place

new york city
so i did nothing
just watched it happen
like all the rest mouths covered
con ed did it
twinsmokestacks belching death
in broad daylight
right in the middle of new york city
in front of all those people
twice in the chest

China Pattern:
an orange potato bug
walks the rim
of my blue willow
rice bowl

wild dog tracks
in the gorge
pads & nail points
& yellow pee
in deer prints
some things salivate
no avoiding it

rooster crowing at the moon
march came in like a maniac
outhouse door sprung a hinge
gotta face town for flour
NO REASON
some things salivate

"...O thank you thank you thank you"

you who wrote the pipers song
you who saved us from our dreary home towns
you who taught us a bum life & a bum death
our Father Jack Kerouac
is gone man
finally high
an empty wine bottle
holding a beautiful candle
"13... this is the knowledge that sees the golden
eternity in all things, which is us, you, me, and which
is no longer us, you me."
thy kingdom come
thou art be done
thank you thank you thank you

POEM FOR SWEET ARTHUR RIMBAUD

although you are but worms
                    you nurture
reborn & thrown
                    thru the dirty window
my home-town mind shattered
in new haven rimbaud
                    verlaine's
traded shots   we all tried-
on the punky mad threadbare
loveaffair suicides
                              Rimbaud
reborn you genderfucker
leaping police barriers
NY 66   you bloody sidewalk
yellow passing line
addicted to the road
itchy Rimbaud walking maniac
climbing the rockies - sierras
-Rimbaud i followed you
up kimono mt.   sweet catskills
Rimbaud soothing herself
suckling mountains Rimbaud
looking to be buggered by angels
Rimbaud hitching out
lower east side acid-bath
hooked on mythic sugardaddys
fled to the deserts
sundrenched smugglers in
moonlit border dashes
guns & weed head north
toward aurora spectacle addict

Rimbaud enough of europes manners
workingclass gypsy crisscrossing
north american wilderness magnet
lures you Rimbaud newfoundland
to sweet rt1 coast road
hitch down to frisco
swim in faggots you a
feathered dike you
Rimbaud reborn Kerouacy
beat chaos cherry wine
no mistaking you for blood Rimbaud
you butch little truck stop
silkyswagger underground Rimbaud
is a knife against the throat
                              of informers
a knife against the throat of time
                              Rimbaud
reborn in the steamroom at the baths
Rimbaud there are thousands of you
riding the shrapnel
like flying rugs

Dirge For The Poets Of Persia
(c.i.a. echo of ghosts in chains in Chile)

all thru the night the land of law & oil is
punctured by machineguns
the army is out breaking up the holymen making
revolution at dawn prayer singers climb high
into minerets & sing to ALLAH ALLAH
& ask their martyrs for the courage to go out again with
the will of allah translated into student chants
today the minaret will serve as a watchtower against tanks
religous rage bred by the monarch of worms & the maggots of civilzation
stashing their millions In swiss banks
& deep within the chambers of the secret police

the interrogators ask the poets to perform
Allah Allah goes thru his mind
& out thru his mouth as aaaAAAHhAHAAAAAAAAAA
the poet in residence in persia
mute gag lil flesh bag containing his testicules
encased in barbwire   he cries
the barbwire in his mouth has his attention
not even screaming is left
the quiet bubbleing of blood
the quiet when all the poets are gone
the quiet after the batlles on the holydays
when tongues are slit to please the shah
behind iron & cement the screams break out
into the streets as
electrodes intrude into his cranium
for writing that article
pills are powdered into his food
that turn revolutionary into lab rat

tat tattle rat tat tat
american trained fascist turns a dial
the poet excretes
to please the shah
more more jets & oil
the shahs wife need a new dress from newyork
no veil she collects warholes
war holes in bodies
I am a persian poet
color me red
& now if i was to go read in tehran or santiago
or a high school in beruit instead of pacific heights
they would attach electrodes to my head
& you sweet innocent students would not exist
no exit
blocked esophogus the quiet bubbling of gone
to please the shah who has tentacles everywhere
oily ducks snowcrystals full of lead
fall like deadheavy eyelids of students
rain on the cemetaries runs red
with the greed of the shah
filling the holydays full of bulletholes

EAGLES

i yearned eagles
& one solstice in the pineforests
island beyond Pelican narrows
sunk like stone
                         tripping   just gone
hadn't moved for hours
it was mosquito mating season
there was a cloud of them 10 ft thick
fucking rather loudly
& too hot to be into our sweat
'cept this dragonfly kept cruising me
in soldier drag kinda on watch
since it dug to chew mosquitos

to death
stood up to a screaming young eagle
squaring a circle my head my little mouse me
totally submissive
it clawed the shit out of my fears
as it dove shrieked 'chee
              chEEEEECHEEEEEEEEE'
screaching & spilt i stumble dazed
had by my first eagle
my other eagles were always more distant
hitching the high coast road cape breton is
              lands
me & the lesbian Rimbaud nosepierced
hanging jewels pierced lots of places
the eagles would glide the thermals cliffside
while we sucked dope from our thumbs
jealous as they tipped a wing & dove the ocean

i hear of the eagle in new york
clawed denim the hook beak parted red
the blackfeather eagle the eagles nest
of studded supple testicle skin
the silver eagle garuda my titsucking eagle
who eats of my heart & spits out my snakes
who flys off with me
i've eaten my share of eagle
i've puked my eagle
been horny for eagle
hitched a thousand miles to cruise just one
        eagle
i've bowed before eagles
lost my breath at their shadows
greatwinged huge wingswath pushing air
eagles - - - - - - wingbeating eagles
that lift me when i'm down eagles
in the possible value of the amerikan eagle
talons in the warplane politicians throats
eagles got babies - - eagles got to eat
            eagles   fly off quick
            gone eagles gone
            on toked eagle vapor

THE BURNING OF PATTI & MICHAEL'S

midnight flames nobody home the roof
toungeing red the walls melting yellow
peter leaping with 6 arms hose snake hard
water rushing the canvas veins sending
big columns of grey smoke the air cold biting
matthew & ralph ripping away clapboards with pulaski's
scraps of burning treasure thrown to the street
no body home but ed warren fighting it like it was
an orphanage
but nobody home nobody hurt nobody burned
nobody lives there anymore...

cold next afternoon
the charred black books
burnt on the shelves
the records melted
the few saved kitchen utensils
Patti & Michael picking thru the
ruins the black roof
the ice on the floor the
strewn charred belongings in the road

the tragedy of flames leaping
the throat chokes
the fates let it be a windless night
such a pretty lil cabin gone-

ME & CODY
(alias Rimbaud)

sittin' on packs
browned in denim
ear rings nose rings
thumbs up
by the side o'the road
from boiceville to a coast
newfoundland - vancouver
jasper elk & blonde morrocan
 oahaccan down pacific
cross again & again
swallow a desert & bake
add more silver rings
bead a brass beat
pack up & gypsy down
along some bar-rail somewhere
goin' somewhere else
hartford fueled us for california

frisco fueled us forever
broken line shootin' on by
me & cody
doing a layback
on the granite slabs
in meat cove
that mule deer mounting her
 the big sur acid beaches
salt etching
tears &
Rimbaud in a gypsy skirt
 oh what a beautiful lesbian
 oh what a roaring fire
we are shooting down some highway
highway - highway

line after line
roadmap dots
truckstop exits
somewhere going
somewhere we   your
extra blanket for tonight
for tonite

CREATION OF THE LIBRARY

average day of
columbian tops &
mexican beer
the literature section
stacked like a
tight sweater
bulging with milk
of newly shelved
porn & beat poets
zen graves - the amerikan
journal of insanity
radio blares - jimmy hoffa dead
denver weather 94
the scuff of a heavy
box of cookbooks
orchestra of a 20 oz. hammer
hand saw/orbital sander
beer zoom - sawdust
& dope cleanings
          the bite
of larkheads on aspen rail
anchored to the guts
of an old piano...
song of carpenters
lust for old beams
inlaid with old imperialist
school maps of asia
still smelling kid dreamy
& the willed remains
of almost dead barry levaas
heaved - shoved - carded
stacked
cordwood waiting
on winter fangs

warm up with
desade & reage
& ginsberg masturbating
old geographics
...liber-gregorian poet
serving espresso &
flowertops
                    to the multitudes
undressing december
to radiator clank
periodically - the horn section
hangout cemetary for the living
dead o' winter - kinda backseat
freefeel
            sci-fi
                        lullabys
of returnables
  anticipating
your fingers
new shelves
eye sucked
handsawed
easy space
stacked tite
easy numbered
definately
the hottest addressbook
            in town
just begging to be had...

ANDY'S HANDS

been breaking down
medievil   torture rack
look at   andy's hands
                      slight cup
                      well scarred
                      rock torn
                      red holes
                      torn scabs
fingers as strong as legs
feet as able as eyes
did ya ever
look at andy's knees?
                      torture maps
                      cut & bruised
                      black & blue
                      rockjock drag
did ya ever dig andy's shoes
well frayed   andy laidback
                      reaching in
                      swollenhead
                      jamcrack
smoking the exhaust of eagles
                      hugging spread
                      flatirons
                      zenbondage
                      did ya ever
see the look in andy's eyes
finding a route thru town
hitching down to climb

The New Firehouse

naked to the waist
7 logs high
chainsaw chewing end butts
dovetail surgery judo lock
& chink - floyd knocks knots off
giant log heave & haul
mixlevel rock wall
hand laid statement
of floyd & steve & mackie
grasping heaving hugging granite
hot sun beating down
sweat & sand mackie naked to the waist
-mixing mortar- wall rises
"working on a buzz. . .
baremuscle swank of carpenters pouches
naked to the waist
stripping bark lifting - heaving
walking blueprint Vale, sets & chinks
great electric screw in stevens hands
bores dowel holes
slam & handsaw
7 logs high
Normans dream of a great vaulted
ceiling before winter
chainsaw shriek dowels slammed
hacking adze sawdust beat
of brushes on a snare
sudden rock soundsplat
pickup bouncing with
ralph throwing rock
naked to the waist
7 logs high
dragon vault o' firefighters
building a lair where quietly lay
the great grunt trucks open-cab
upfront gutrub with the forces of fire . . .

dream yearning pole chinking
dues meeting smell of coffee
brewing benefit breakfasts
same folks chewing up fire line
with pulaski's & spade
drawing the line
collectively dealing with horror
of black trees and smokey remains
same folk peter & fuzzy
sunday morning seeking donations
yellow hardhats & showy truck
same folks here tonight dousing
out the hot vibes o' feds
the new firehouse
collective revolution
working on a buzz
people muscle
matthew-floyd-bill-steve-ralph-mackie-mark
7 logs high
& naked to the waist
the poetry ends
the dance begins
rubbing til we ignite
get hot now
spontaneous combustion
up goes the firehouse...

Ed The Maintainer Man

high   above the dustthenoise
seasons of ice & slush
pushing his luck in mythical machine
scraping the great up & down
earphones & maybe a kid
the ultimate public servant
giving time he is plowing a driveway
hauling a sucker out on his chain
doing russian roulette with sawmill hill
he's a hell of a fella
pushing his luck
high   on the ballfield
pushing pebbles & boulders
up & down the canyon
day & nights too bad for the bar
we're inside looking out the window
at familiar roarings
as the big blade of willpower
stops for a break
& he hauls out a guitar
makes love with a fiddle
then back on the big wheels
up & down the canyon
high   above the dust the noise
pushing back the nasties
no matter what the season
us living here his reason
the ultimate public servant
bouncing in his cab
up & down the canyon
no matter what the weather
pushing back the nasties
in all the places he doesn't have'ta
high   above the regulations

bouncing in his cab
up & down the canyon
no matter what the weather
pushing back the nasties
in all the places he doesn't have'ta
high   above the regulations

From The Boulder County Justice Center

corrections

she ust'a be a skinny speed freak
pills again her probation officer got her
"indeterminate" at the funny farm pueblo
she came back for a brief visit
court in boulder yesterday
she lost both her kids 15 & 12
she's fatter takes her pills
 -takes her pills- that's what they put her away for
but   that's justice

                  family fight victor did months
                  got out got in on rape she said
                  she made it up - got out again
                  last week he killed his brother-
dykes dykes in jail imagine that
boulder liberals shudder
can't have that
put all the women in security
isolation no poetry
they busted her with contraband;
a comb & knotted sheet an article
"how to stay young jumping rope"
in her 60's worked 10hours a day in the laundry
published the paper but getting extradited
no longer a model prisoner
               again
jim & i will stay in touch thru the ward library
getting seperated in salt lake city soon
jim gets crippled with fates shadow
gonna do time at 60
gonna lose his wife
for laundering mafia bread
afro & ring thru his nose

rapping about slave names
& innocence & public defenders
correction
public defenders act as garbagemen
it's one of those bad periods in jail
when the guards are bucking for results
& the inmates are coming back
recidivists boomerang back again
for pickin' off the university cops eyes
is what he writes about in the workshop
rehearses with friends a play but only at breakfast
cause green module can't see blue module can't hang out
with gold or red and trustees and women can't take part
permission to use plastic silverware civilian clothes
guitars & poets from the mountains...
just outside over the wall bulletproof liberal
prison but no poetry for women & none for him, he bad
in come medicine
with sugary nurse
giving it all out
free
pushing dope
in our workshop
watch poets
 shuffle up
 & swallow
drowning themselves
while trying t'
ignite the night

OM MONEY MONEY MONEY

"Do not rely on individuals, rely on the teachings.
   Do not rely on the words, rely on the meaning.
   Do not rely on the adapted meaning, rely on the ultimate meaning.
   Do not rely on intellectual knowledge, rely on wisdom." -
                                    The Dalai Lama

a line of monks in maroon & silks
the low chanting begins
om money money money
Karmapa got a gunfighters rep
don't look that fast
but usedt'a cakes & bucks
masochist kneelers
i put out my feelers
cruising a chubby monk
with an armload of souvenirs
blue surge vajra goons
they're everywhere bookstore bakery
lookin lil' looser than in hemerroid temple
puja was hot - thighbone trumpets & pretty grunting
fronting for the buddha
with guards in mercedes
doormen - doberman attitudes
the buddha who fears an attack
a simple shuck for a hundred grand
   meanwhile a disciple attacks
tests the guru a bit
dharma combat & now the koan
how to come up with $10,000 dollars bail
as easily as boulder vomits up a dowery
thousands of silks
thousands fuel the hype
hip red-neck strings dig deep
mahayana mafia picking up the take
the boys in ties looking harvard
gotta peddle the light
infiltrate the achievers before they die
shooting up tibetian transfusion of aristocratic illusions

om money money money
i hear it
i hear it
the lotus opens slowly like bank vault
the jewel is jive
can't buy it
gotta share it
not sell shares
MANI descends t'Money
PADME t'Pad me
Om t'Boom
the sound of steel doors locking
the temple as ant farm
false alarm
light but no fire
cold cash
disarmed
un harmed
refined
refied
confined
concenration campy
armored carpets
kinda touchy at the temple these days
we blow a big columbian heresy outside
cruise t'puja past the guards
hey, is he with you
no suit no tie
sit on red mat
karmapa jamming with the monks
things change
the monks trance into maroon skunks
his Holiness begins t'molt
sangha gets a jolt
as his face changes to Big Daddy Idi Amin
reborn in boulder ruler for life
blank check lama
a shoulder t'cry on

a path t'die on
the hitchhikers of light
paying on a mercedes
strung out on capitalist rabies
mad dogs in silk
hock a very expensive nothing
void of superstars
in nice cars
the dharma rebate is coming
says so in the tibetian book of the media
telling how to buy time on installments
in cancer cells
in jail cells
chogyams attacker in the local hell
while bald maroon imports dine
the kid eats time
impaled on the light in his cell
lama called the cops
wanna have a dokusan behind bulletproof glass
with bodyguards & meditation cages
the rage bottled begins t'rot
as mad dogs in silk do puja
in a neurotic hockshop
the stench of rotting meat invades
a chubby monk with rabies
puts the bite on for the bucks
like an undercover catholic
chanting OM MONEY MONEY MONEY
OM MONEY PAD ME LUCK
horney believers dig deep
black hat superhooker
while
somewhere in the ghetto
avolokitsvara starves
with a thousand arms
covers ears
while the chant goes on
OM MONEY MONEY MONEY

PEAK T'PEAK GESHIA

white cranes fly off brown silk
kimono suckershot from guns
of feds of beds raided

a quick change into fryes
tite levis freeway
lullaby out cruising
punky threadbare fireside

the whispered wantings of
mountain boys
confide in a geshia's ear
how they pine away
the fire fed
hungers flame
time bites

the geshia sits alone
with smoking pipe
in her room
playing her stringed thing
weaving to the beat
of her own heart

she burns his old straw sandels
making tea for her new lover
who is about to come
herself
she sits rocking
upon scrimshaw whaletooth
worn smooth
making music
in the moonlight
snowscape
white clean wind blowing
peak t'peak

Hic-Coo

lentini at dusk
on horseback
white denim
wandering switchback
sky apricot
it's clear
baby picks up rhythm
of a horse
lentini looks fellini
olive dark open
ripe
out riding
lullabying
dark quiet
smiling
baby turning
inside her

Looking Down Lefthand

from gateway
eddie warren
broadbrimmed
chizeled walk
carbide hat
& his pick
levis historically
a local man knowing
the veins running thru town . . .
tripod mutts
chase brother dave
big yellow payloader
dragging tail
long day over
home from boulder
checking the mail

HERE COMES THE JUDGE

Friday evening when the lights melt away
a peoples paradox walks up the hill
justice goes in drag
sneakers a jacket & tie
about t'give a black eye
t'turkeys who say
"this ain't real-
you have no right to..."
do you have a licence to use that gun
but it ain't quite fun
the peoples paradox don't pout
just gets loud & serious
make defendants delerious
this is a court of law
you have the right to a fair trial
a lawyer & one of three choices
guilty-   notguilty-   or no contest
which is the same as guilty
under our municipal laws
you could possibly receive
a $300 dollar fine and 90 days in jail

it's quiet now
they're just lookin a little pale

Gid calls them up   checks ID
& they enter their plea
& unwind their drivel

"Sir you must listen to my story
the officer must have been wrong -
i've been a boyscout for 26 years
my sons are boyscouts -
i love the scouts sir & the officer giving me
the ticket even had a boyscout shirt on -

please take these facts
into consideration in my fine sir-"
"of course i will
 i find you guilty- $25 plus $13 over
(the speed limit) plus $6 in court costs
please pay the clerk $44 - thank you next -
"Not guilty sir- just wish my fuzz-buster was working..."
-guilty pay the clerk next please!-

the old woman in an uproar about how this couldn't be real
the real folks who cop to going too fast for our kids
the cop sweating it out all day eating dust to keep blood off
the road   blood off the road   blood off the road
compassion is a double edged blade & we've already had too
many close shaves - as a jeep with hippies goes thru the
stopsign at 50
just missing a kid & Scoop Dubitsky
leaps out with a sidekick into it
brakes squeel & some freak raises up a bottle & justice was
bruce & pat & the boys quietly sittin in front of the store just
watching & waiting & listening to a potential
killer bitch
 so friday evening as the lights melt away
& strange pickups pull into town with speeders scowling
the peoples paradox walks up the hill
with the word   justice
feeling just fine just fine

ON PAWNEE PEAK

from Isabel
                    big gulp of ginsing
                    the glacier slips
                    aqua melt into the lake
thunderheads & cold breeze
a thousand feet of lousy teeth
divide claws bluevoid
reaching out peak to peak
              rockyclock - sun
crumbles snow walls
wind eats rock walls
pika shit
 footprints
   kicked steps
    bugs pecked
    by snowfield
     nameless black birds
thin air
              park laws?
maybe utes reborn in ward
wovacas prophesy
buffalo return shaggy
bring peace in new form
of fuzzy bob - town star...
peak to peak thoughts
buttercups & dead avalanches
peaking we raise the
flag- she stands atop the cabin
wearing his underwear-
sit & toke
 thin air

counting breathes
holding hands
peak to peak
the sound of rock
ripping wind
taut thighs
thoughts wing
peak to peak
with ghostly scuff
of mocassin

Aspen Roots Once Yanked-
The Heads Of Deer

a heavy sweater wet with fog
limp yellow leaves
push & prod
weathersleathers &
a most able master
whips me up the hill again
rope up an armload of deadwood
& shoulder it out
again-
        again & pile
sweat - drink & walk up
again & again
the cold fog whispering
more - more oh more
        out back i lusted
the brown peel the blonde
aspens so wonderfully dead
the chainsaw screaming
back at the master
more - more again & again
the shoulder aches so nice
the legs taut
downhill mind coils & snaps
& i whip up the hill once more

Sitting

window
moonlight
pull up shade
take seat
deep bite
silver
kindling
spirit
clean echo
falls thunk
turned crystal
motionless heave
oceans of notions
too rotten
to make much heat
but the hardwood
window frame
burns well &
next burns
chopping block
bananas
sex
am i doing it right?
o.k.
start again
count out breaths
3
4
back pain
5
knees ow
mouth dry
again
1
2
dead
3

count both breaths
monk junk
fried
345
stoke the fire
567
ashes never turn
to ashes
present tense
footprints
snow path
somebody
dusted
my axe

CURLED ALONE I FALL INTO DREAMING

pines murmuring
& we tongue & grooved
amid the toss & turnings
on a cold mountain night
the yearnings for warmth & wet

we warped slightly
from rainy past nights
& couldn't fit as tite

a choir of coyotes yapping on a hill
our eyes opened
their throaty barking
a departure from my habits
it's a new time
nothing matters so much
i don't care about you
more than ever

'Coyote'- the union of whores in frisco...
from the doorway of my heart
amid the toss & turnings
amid the hungry yearnings
i empty the pockets of my life
for coyotes i give it all

& we fell again
til a knife of half moon
pulled back our lids
and i was home for a while
the baby crying never sounded
so good so sweet til the
dawngong rosey
you & the baby
hiking into town for school
& the coyotes laid up somewhere
curled together furry ball
of things meshing
together at the right time
i fall back into dreaming

ULTIMATE CAPITALIST DEATH BREATH
a poem for sam cohen
of the RAND corp.
inventor of the neutron bomb...

it wasn't enough to have the firepower
of a burning planet
no war was hell on the victors budget
cost so damn much to rebuild japan
germany & italy sucked our dollars dry
it took the fun out of a good war...
sam worked hard in his lab
then went to the pentagon to peddle his wares
teach them damn soviets to play techobutch with us...
sam had a clean atomic bomb
lil blast & a few things blown but mostly
the silent neutron dandruff
more like being gassed than blasted
nixon fueled the program
while selling pepsi to moscow
& sipping tea with mao
james sleschinger former head of the CIA
now head of energy for carter
hid the bomb in the water budget
tucked in between paper damns
millions of dollars
                        to kill humans & animals
to penetrate the soft tissues
but not hurt the gold
not break the machines
leave the glass intact in the windows
in moscow & new york

neutron warheads on cruise missles
backed by jimmy carter
rapping about how much he loves bob dylan
echo of " a hard rain gonna fall...
selling ultimate death breath to NATO
kill them fuckers without hurting one painting
who cares about who's there
little neutrons don't care
fly through the air a predictable distance
then settle into the hearts & lungs...
sam cohen is a family man   a PhD
just earning a living
working for the energy czar
from cia to whitehouse
                    rancid peanutbutter breath
& he won't quit smiling & announcing
"work was already underway to develop
a non-atomic trigger like laser..."
no blast   no heat   just death breath
greed bomb putting out 8-10,000 rads of death
when it takes but 650 to kill
by enhanced radiation
next step in riot control

sit
       holding my own hands
breathing
      in
           out
              in

                  out
                     you come
                  like water
                  downstream
                  splashing
                  hello & good-bye

                  then another
                     mourning
                  outside the present
                  for that which isn't
                    NOW
i think of smelling

                  daffodils & young
                  marijuana
morning glorys heavenly blue
& watch the clouds tattoo
the sky
         the wind erases

BURN SCARS MAKE
PRETTY MEADOWS/AWFULLY

silver hardhats piled for lunch
chainsaws bathe in oil
noon peanutbutter butch corral
the boys laidback for lunch
swapping lies about thighs
tipping canteens & looking
for things to steal- a meal
of dyed red pine corpses
bark beetle larve tanfade
greenscream gagged ridges
manmeddle chainsaw officially
tagged in deathbag red
by the U.S. Forest Service
me & jean & jim cannon
so dry a smile too hot
meadows of hay & tourists dropping butts
lightening gonna deliver ol red cream pie
dante dinner eating chili & cherry reds
while the joint is in flames
we are carpetbag firewatchers pyromaniacs
purple asters puckerups cannibis
japradish beegong (my mind runs across 7th ave.
holding a slice)   dipstick
bow'ry poets down a quart
aquarian age umbilical bondage
eyes in the back of our heads
blank fronts & high pressures
meeting cold receptions
airplanes hit the mountains
all the time   sloppy TV suture
by burgular white collared hood
frogeggs in aspenslime
columbine   hummingbirds

duck rain/dangerous abandoned mines
in our skulls the scarred hillsides
old tailings naked
'cept for those lone clinging pines
fools gold everywhere
amazon mushrooms
haunting splendor
history hereabouts - yellow fever
fools gold graveyard
haunting splendor
sucked backwards thru a pneumatic tube
like dept store charge account-
lone cinderblock in the weed
the bomb already went off
the bomb already went off
clockstopper firepuke red dandruff
saltshaker cayanne from a B-52 1976
- i repeat, be on the lookout for a B-52   1976
plutonium
accident
armed
to
the
tits
of
hiroshima
burn
scars
meadow
of
ashes
pretty
awful
dust
to

kick.

NIGHT BONES

what made you so appealing
decayed like fish
wrapped in newsprint-
the old words came alive
and devoured us with
our own hungers

i put my arms around you
you became curtains
in a funeral parlor
with the window open
damp & cold with the
lid left open
all night

i leaked
a watering can full of blood
you ate the garden dirt
& shit worms
birds ate our eyes
magpies fought jays
to break our eardrums
mice run from my mouth
ticks settle in my pits
my leg rots at a wierd angle
an elk walks across my mouth
the brain has gone to maggots
with this terrible stench

the final bowl of skull
lay crushed & dripping
noisy rats fight over our tongues
sun boiled flesh like moldy bread
strewn garbage on barbed wire

& so it ends
a dump fire
crushed backpacks
broken whiskey glass
stale cake
head thru windshield
accidental teenage red
radio ghost of jealous love songs
vomitdrip
dry & dead

IN PREPARATION FOR TEACHING
NOTHING AT A BUDDHIST UNIVERSITY

the wind is the only sure thing tonight
jupitar stares hard
the outline of burnt mt.
& a candle to type by
hot stove with soup
& neverending suckershots
blow on by
grab the silver ring
& hock it for a ticket anywhere

  turn back on the edge
  return
  ripped tide
she predicted my death at 32
a bullet thru the head
in a cave
shacking up with the ghost
of lew welch

just to be able to let go

going to lecture on
spilled soup
flophouse poetry
sung by
truck slave
dishwasher
ditchnigger
runaway slave

turned whore
with friends in jail
poems in the mail
emptypocket brokenheart
to deal with start
by sweeping out
all this vulture vomit

just to be able to let go
the stove making ashes
of willing aspen

only to be able to let go
of never ending suckershots

DOING TIME, LONG TIME IS LIKE PAINTING LAYER UPON LAYER OF LAQUER ON A HOT ROD - BUT NO ENGINE - GOING NOWHERE SO YA PINSTRIPE THE POSSIBILITIES FOREVER TILL YA GET YOUR OWN LEGS BACK

they were 17& bitchin' candyapple Irish white &
riding their bikes   a chip off the old block
selling weed to the rich kids at Fordam

hit a drugstore a gas station sold some
weed & toy guns but didn't matter
busted & sent away t'prison   irish white & bitchin
gonna straighten out their minds   did some time
lost first bout with the board
instead of parole got a transfer to a bigger hole

they were riding down the highway in a prison car
three prisoners & two guards
so nice to be out riding
chuck gary & buddy two guards Fitzgerald & Bowerman
riding down the thruway   nice day a lil change
everything was going nice but ol buddy had tried escape
twice & while cigarettes & conversation drifted
buddy was cutting cutting cutting
a razor blade thru leather security belt buddy was cutting
buddy just wanted t'cut out so bad
buddy was cutting real quiet cutting ever since they left
buddy needed t'cut so bad   one hand   two
he shows chuck & gary still tied
buddy throws his hands around guards neck
grabs his gun blam blood spatters around the car
sliding across the thruway the other guard kills buddy

car screeched to a stop stop stop
but guard fires anyway & gut boil red
legs kick up spastic to save the head
stop! stop! & when they did
they called it a conspiracy to murder
gave them the waiting room for the chair
but it never got t'do their hair
they became an issue in the sixties fighting to grow
hair & beard behind thirty ft. walls
bitchin' candyapple as possible 'poeming painting
trying t'dry a mamas tears find a decent lawyer
don't give up don't let the long nights in a tiny cell
wear ya out   don't freak at wakin behind bars
sit & wait   electric bait
in the last ten years going on trial three times
on same charges   first trial a hung jury
 the second in the death sentence followed by a
unanimous reversal and the third -
in a sentence of twenty-five t'life
after twelve long years of endless nights
lawyers families revolutionaries lovers
newspaper reporters video radio and publiclty attack
a heart attack in ink tryin t' make the public think
but the judge lets them sit & wait
& so we visit thirty ft. walls open & swallow
us into Greenhaven State Prison
no more poetry workshops here
so I pad tite levis with thin potent onionskin
smuggeling in poetry past metal-detectors
past infrared stamps past steel doors past steel guards
in hallway entrance t'visitors room
she's just leaving kissing goodbye
"honey next week send me some knits"
hugs waves & jogs down the hallway with tears in his eyes
visitors room is big yellow chairs plastic everywhere

kids running around   lovers trying t'feel flesh & lips
cameras spray the room with intrusion
hugs waves & jogs down the hallway with tears in his eyes
visitors room is big yellow chairs plastic everywhere
kids running around   lovers trying t'feel flesh & lips
cameras spray the room with intrusion
gray weary matron acts like usual nothing going on
people are desperatly trying t'make love
in front of soda machines coffee machines
 sandwich machines
old father visiting his son can't hold back the tears

screaming across the room   gary & I hugging
something thicker than blood between us
"how are things in the mountains
I cant believe you're a judge
sneak any poetry in?
he looks at her   it's classic
she's a journalist from Woodstock
he says "hi tomata" hey man does that sound sexist?
after being in 12yrs I know what a tomata is"
says closed down poetry workshop   too political
can't fight them head on gotta survive
dig this   this is my politics for now
i got a secret weapon
i got a real street hotplate not homemade
so dig we organise our block
76 guys mostly black & spanish
i get food together every nite from commisary & packages
but of course they're ain't no cooking allowed
i got rice & beans going
frying some beautiful garlic & onions in a tin can
oh man it just smelled so beautiful oh man you dont know
just how good
man everybody getting high off the smell in the cellblock

56

but the hack smells it too & comes down to put the bite on
us but my man BJ the lifter is out & tells the hack
hey man you want another attica?
we're willing to go down for our right to more than slop
it ain't homemade booze or dope so fuck off hack
& besides you get fed first every nite   ok man you first
just relax & we'll call ya when its ready
& gary keeps cooking & feeding different guys every nite
share some smoke & talk talk talk how t'make it better
wash the tin cans out & clean it up   stash plate
work out a deal for longer showers
bribe the guards with anything that works
like a real hotplate & a decent shower

gary is actually sucking peg's toe
right there in the visiting room
says ya know i swing a lot of weight here but
this man, this freaked the boys out last visit
& it feels so good i'm gonna do it some more
tell them people in the mountains i'm coming on out tell
them citypunks oh man the things i gotta do with peg
running thru the fields man i just gotta get out"...

but for xmas 1978 the n.y.s. supreme court turned them
down & they won't even come up before them again
for 13 more years more years more years more years
days minutes ticking off so slow
in a cell 6'X 8'
chewing on their fate

THE WIND IS A HOOD/THE SNOW
IS A CHEAP TEASE

shreds of plastic sail by
drunken wind in a knife fight
with the boards on the house
- blankets morn the moon
hanging over drafty glass
it's 'bout -10 & nobody
too far from their stove
ponderosa beetlekill
fire at will
sweet lithe dead aspens
bring out necrophyliac
pyromanic   lust for dead wood

the wind is a hood
snow is a cheap tease

the crystals hanging
shatter the kitchen with rainbow
dance of cowboy coffee
            morning homegrown
            radio free jazz
            chickadees blowing on by
            soprano exits from pinewoods
                        the reed section is composed of
                              peruvian import
                              snore storm
                              seal song on an ice flow
                              Orbit dog barking

the tin side of the shaft stutter
the shreaded corrugated roof chimes
a lone coyote sniffs the tailings
wanders the ruins of gold
"nothing to eat here"

splits pneumatic paws
a sly ballet out the backdoor of town

the post office is full of pregnant
things to come
winter orgaz of bare lightbulbs
                    sucking sounds
                    gotta keep the mothers hot
            fleshfule fools gold
            loveaffairs with no front
                            no back
                            can't remember
                            a place to end
                            the wind keeps blowing
    silk & wool insulate the thighs
    a fool is a thing without a hat
stories from the east float in
bitching wet cold lots of snow but
glad i'm back"
                    altitude is holiday
                    heavy metal kids glow
                    alternate space program
                    the power of a million free baggies
                    the weapon of volume
                    badmouthing amerika
                    dividing
                    multiplying
                    adds up to neighbor hoods
                            understoods
                            slain fences
stoned Quixotes worshipping windmills
glassed gardens
sticky resinous clits of hairy female flowers
the boys worshipping the motherlode
a deep vein of buddha's afterbirth
                    babyshit
                    Depot credit
                    umbilical radio announces

another tanker broke up in a storm off the coast
two men climb the wet cold mountains of the bottom
the government has ads on the tube
jimmy carter   jimmy carter does outcast drag
blue denim secret service peanut freak
...beards are no longer allowed in Argentina
cleanshaven identity cards a must
but up here even for the cops
the wind is a bust

> balls of crystal hang ups
> tales of coast t'coast
> cardoors packed with dope
> weekends packed with hope

snowstuds on glare ice perform
impossible peak t' peak testy
tirades coming down off niwot
but button up getdown live band
at the Pioneer bearclaw fastdraw
wanna dance wanna beer wanna?
do a spring wiporwill
wanna wip?
abandoned arms flail hips
drums moan the ass goes berserk
the bass throbs the spine jellies out
saturday night Kundalini
dances the cobra
dances a tongue from a hood
of levis basket
Cuervo fools gold
mouth t' mouth
shotgunned rush
at band break
-10
a knot of friends untie
one on one on one
the barren wind swept rock by the Atlantic
hitchhikes ending in surf - careless sea birds
pea-coat & black cap   that was the past

the cost of the will   roots grow around stone
deep down taking time
people rapid submission   it has happened here
sad eyes & bloody noses   unable to drive   anywhere
friends dug fred out of a cave-in   it was dark
& six hours of digging deep   digging deep thoughts
fred wore his fingertips off digging his way out
while friends were digging in -
alkoloids have us buzzing   stars spit on us
look it up   like a good shower
the berzerk boxer sleeps in jail   sad tales tell
the moon t'reflect on the shadows   cost analysis of a
clean towel - tried in tested ways
thick stars eating rich deserts
after winning the heat at the Garden
black gladiators in satin trunks bruised eyes cut
lips   sad hips   lube tube   blown top   lost cool
mellow cop psycho stereo   lewd antennae topless
dancer in a trance   don't trust him
too many travelling scars

from ricepaper 8 X 21
Greg Tebrich collection

Meditation

the hitch
the burro pulls
the wheels turn
the man sits still
he gets there
but not alone
what ever
ends in s
is home
for instance
like incense is silent
roads wind
noise curves
for instants
clowns
alaska
all governments
bulls eye
lizards tongue
every form of fishing
midnight
space capsules
Sandoz & N.A.S.A.
shamans
shemens
for instants
spider webs
nets
lonely poets
totem poles
salads

populations
rations
orgies
goings on
roses
thorns
thistles
noon whistles
lottery tickets
prayers to god
dozen eggs
tomatoes
getting spaced with a friend
what ever
ends in S

last of the summer folks
going to seed
the phallic mullen
erect & furry
red clover browning droopy
tired caraway
naked milkweed
late day
going to seed
to seed the sun
blue sky going to seed
 mosquitos
freeze blunt
blood thickens
bran muffins &
bruised peaches
last o' the summer folks
alone rocker going off
in a taste o' coming winds
the green things bend heavy
toward hay

        aspen sweet yellow
pale pale

        jailed by the weather
        you become a snow horny
        winter hermitage;
        the ptarmigan all white
        feet feathered
        climbing just above
        the treeline - once
        in a while maybe a blink
        shortlived tracks
        in windswept snow

pale pale clockcold cabinsmoke
        mariciabo & homegrown
last o'the summer folks
        going to seed
        pale smoke as he
        bends foward
        over a baggie
        getting off his rocker
            stonewall
            gone to weed

Frozen

lake don't care about the moon
just another passing ball
& a lover that goes home early

WANTED

poem for cameron bishop

poem for those who refuse to talk
poem for susan sax trapped inside
the collapsed mine of doing time
poem for bernadine dorn
& underfriends burrowing tunnels
deep enough to undermine
moles armed with light
sitting tite & printing
moving fast & merging
the roots of tinder
unable to forget
villages in cinders
mi lai
boston   detroit
faces pressed in horror
against bus windows
white adults hurling rocks
at black 6 year olds
WANTED for 6 1/2 years
masquerades nights alone
nights hiding fires
days dodging planes
WANTED in every postoffice gallery
WANTED in every personnel office file
as bearded beat blackturtlenecked
weatherfolk with wires hanging from
his teeth..........moving moving
underground with the eyes of
10,000 feds looking down
all around with the
eyes of border guards
of rhode island

border guards of colorado
the eyes of prision guards
stareing deep
change up keep moving always moving
still the rent   still food
WANTED right forearm
tatoo -skunk holding mirror-
burnt off with glowing cigarette
moving moving
up the trail to isabel
no bugs 'cept the ones biting
no one watching but the peaks
cam & mary sitting in fireweed
WANTED yes WANTED more & more
picture hanging in the postoffice
WANTED IN WARD
WANTED for the rest of your life
....the moles are organizing
burrowing burrowing   eating thru
doors making senators fear
where they piss
washington is going yellow
underneath it all
lights from the underground
blowing out
the evidence
blowing out the lights
in grand jury chambers
making the wanted WANTED
making the not wanted WANTED
WANTED a poem
WANTED; A POEM FOR CAMERON BISHOP
sung by a chorus of twelve
not guilty not guilty not guilty not guilty not guilty not
guilty not guilty not guilty not guilty not guilty not guilty
not guilty   BUT WANTED

PENNY POKER

what a smoker
blue deck
regular back   but up front
where it counts
where the pot is high
stakes are high
mostly women   nobody shy
anyway they're with this
porney deck
       ace bets darling
       i'll bump it one
       the ace got em
       going down on her
       5 o'spades up the ass
       2 o'hearts sidesaddle
(tall bob, hands on the table!)
       i'm in i'm in me too
       flush of screws
            oh yes, a fine deck
       a long dick
       a stacked deck
       cut & shuffle
           6's suck
           pair of queens going down
       pennies stacked
       everybody wins
       peepshow   bob's trick nines
           raise you two blowjobs
           bumping
           it's hard
           trash t'the left

pass the joint
dara's fivers bumpin' two
susie's got an orgy in her hands
10 of spades lickin' dick
you in you in you in???
three of a kind
flushin jacks are better
let her fold
uranus in gemini first house
your deal

YOUR SHORTS ARE OUR BUSINESS

The HUM   the honk   the spin
of wire brushes grease lushes
humping greasy starter parts
worn brushes busted nuts
the damaged shaft
drips black-test red
stader dead-
                    the rich kids pour in
back t'school
wanting to know why their
idiot light won't go off...
shop filled with wounded foreigners
V.W. volvo saab stories
& the lameduck detroits
doing annual cashregister obsolete
with the owners leased
to their wallets
expecting a.j. foyt & a bit of freud
at welfare rates having
telephone catharsis
"mister, my blinkers are broken
my parking lights gone
the oil light's on
there's a funny smell
coming outta the radio
but it shouldn't cost much
i fixed it myself just a few
days ago...
                    hello "auto electric
hello auto electric- hello yes
we do...WHAT? hold on
WHAT? Yes ma'am..........

the compressor going BRAMMMMMMMMMMM
BRAMMMMMMMMMM the air rachet
gives her the hatchet WRRRRRRRRRRRR
WRRRRRRRRRYES MA'AM
the amp meter bouncing
the growler flashing
phone ringing
horn beeping
                boss rolling a fat one
tie-dyed joggin from bench t'car t'
toolwagon back & forth beeping YES MA'AM
...joe just legs sticking out neath a truck
gary upside down rewiring big Cummings
with cab flipped over
burnt bulbs
AC-DC power beams
full field fried
the grounded socket to my
heart
blisters the heat-shrink tubing
t'my brain
i fall for a blue toyota
with some hot shorts

MUCKING THE COLUMBIA

her greyhair dreamings of someday
reopening
                slide like wetheavy dirt
Mackie blasts away, picking &
dumping, Stevie heaves a barrowfull
while Matthew readys a transfusion
of logwall
                to keep a ghost dancing
in the ol hotel...
shreds of lace curtain wave
oak veneer curls
disabled old rockers recall
the lovebounce in the bridal suite
now mirrored in bugspit &
peeling wallpaper
steel shoehorn
beaded dress on the velvet loveseat
an old Rocky Mtn, Times-1935-aug. 7th
"Idleness seen as a menace to youth"
sink of saints... dust
the upturned bones of a horse
the lovebounce returns
as mackie blasts away
as fuzzy packs a wall
shorin' up the dream
which was the milkglass doornob
to the loveseats gossip
of hotlove being sewn
in the ol Columbia
her greyhair dreamings
in barrows full
the gossip of gone workers
falls on the shoulders
of mackie&matthew&steven mucking

SHROVE SUNDAY

pancakes before lent
eddie warrens stove
     is 79 years old
stacks of buckwheat & sourdough sizzle
as patty pours out more
& coffee's endless rounds of joints passed annointing
a snowy day in town
               with a big kitchen
               full of stories
"there's worms around here that's psychedelic—
—gotta smoke 'em when they're fresh—
—course, it ain't easy lighting up a wet worm...

THEY LOVED EACH OTHER SO MUCH

she drank beer out of his wooden leg
& stalked the innocent around the bar
making some squelch at the foaming foot
while the ludes fell freely down her throat
& romance burned like what
if someone showed up to visit
someone lonely
with a cakebox of plutonium
    rose
    black glowing
    plutonium rose
bloom upon thy neck
the lip prints of a friend
so hot that baby breath wilts
at the sight of you
with a guitar slung
lowrider truckstop
cheap whores slopping down runny eggs
    toast on brownbuds
    eyebrows rocking
    "oh i'm in so damn deep baby"
    she cooed
    but the shoe flew
    & hit a beautiful man
    on the nose
    & all the roses in the world
    wilted
    and that's how broken hearts reveal
    storm bent sparrows
suckershots they land gratefully & feed
on black plutonium roses
& shit little threats
of lovers holding on
clinging to the fabric
of timewoven hours a patchwork quilt of flowers
before they bombed out

The Longing

you never knew
i stole
one silver hair
tied it round
round my cock

since you've gone
only my black
turtleneck feels right

on nights like this
windy & cold
you a 1000 miles away
in the city
me trying t'use
love poems
as extra blankets

thinking 'about you
taking back your hair
build a nest
lay my head t'rest

Thinking About The Winter Whore
Whitehair Lady Of Winter   Blo

broken glasses on the highway littered with broken hearts
a car that wouldn't start & a threeway abandoned
a snort & a punchy jukeboke with a discharge
invisible
walk home
the first blizzard blowing in
the first real california sinsimilla blowing in over the divide
the referee in the mercedes
the mercy of the quiet ones
home in bed with the kids asleep
and the firewood stacked
& the shelves full of food for thought
enuf to last thru 20 blizzards
& all the lights off in town
'cept for the stores' & insomniac writers
telltale smudges on the mirror
which is never on the wall anymore
off the wall of rock cold snowbite white swirl
comes t'town like some wonderful girl
willing to be everybodys lover
whether ya like it or not
the moon is in trouble
littered with broken hearts
soon t'be covered with a million grams of the best
snow will replace snow
winter won again
the long walk from the bar
with yer gloves lost somewhere on the floor
gonna jump between a lot of covers
if ya can make the corner near the welders house
where the mountain tests your weight & yer hat
oh yeah
gonna make two tracks downhill screaming
the mirror covered the powder
& you leaping thru it

HOME GROAN

pines bent in homage to the first snow
smoke curling out of breakfast
paths chopped on the morning mirror
pastry & coffee & joints & coffee & joints & coffee
& mail & coffee somewhere joints & boots & gloves
from house to house hats & joints & coffee &
chop & split & hang close t'the stove & heat water
& invent chores to forget roll another one
just like the other one

"i haven't got laid in weeks - i deserve it
& he's so handsome - wish he would just ask me out."

& roll another one
just like the other one

beat the bag
get the old bindings ready
wetdream winter water
& roll another one

gimme another shot another beer another
just like the other one roll one
til the great nasal blizzard of '78
blew into town in a white cadallac with white
ermine seats with a white driving studly white walls
& white chinook sealskin wallet on the way to the bank
on the good ole game of 8-ball late night wind howling
down off niwot gimmee another one roll one

"shit! where the fuck are all the women
what kind   a frontier is this anyway
anybody got a joint?
a spare sister? a bag full of liver? abuddy
about to become a drunken feel   anybody
anybody   shit   goodnight boys"
go home & roll another one
just like the other one
trying t'get higher
in the one-way mirror
with nobody behind it.

NAMELESS ANGEL
for Aslheigh Cannon

a rumor in the eveing
on a night the town was aglow with coca & pupils
halo of mumbo wafting above the highballs
dropping down the pockets
          rumor
          contractions every 60 seconds
                  heavy breathing
                  push comes t'shove
                  all night long long
the wise men came in from another gulch
bringing baggies of herb & fantastic powders
their eyes long gone gone on little blotter dragons
their hopes inhaled & blown braided into a nesting place
while you   nameless angel
changed lanes   long 'bout dawn
                with your mama pushing down
                lil' submariner
                waiting for the light
                breaking thru the water
                with your mama pushing down
                & yer daddy wildeyed
                & the wise men & the women
                    calling you out
                  & the midwife was a man
              in the season of the flowers
                unfolding in the dawn
                  come-along
                  come-along
                the sun needs a daughter

& yer mama just needs t'get smaller
while you were working it out
shooting stars signaled
the change from saline t'sweet
nameless angel
the one we all been waiting for
                    your aunt rode around screaming
                        "it's a girl - "she's born"
                        & the wisemen sat laughing
                        heavy lids & hollow noses
                        & contemplated breakfast
& in the morning yer mama hit the depot
like some chinese lady off to work
after plowing the soil all night long long
big belly pushin & shovin big breathing - yer daddy
wildeyed
your aunt roaring   & yer mama unfolding her —
come-along
 come-along
            coca dawn
                    the one we all been waiting for —
just a rumor in the evening   &   a miracle this morning

PORTRAIT OF A PAINTER
for Jeane Pless

in black straps
on sized linens
taking a rap
wet into wet
sunshaft
slowstroke
bit o'smoke
entering herself
thick bush
brush stroking
the bones of a closed pussy
aborting white wounds-
paintbrush sutures
the wound of a crippled couple
a mother screaming
from child abuse
she gets loose
painting opened mouths dripping
the past skinned & butchered
cadmium red brush rag
art the gilded hag
dripping its last period
doctor television prescribes
bribes sketched in
bank lines
passbooks tokens the tongues
longed for silence
the end of bloody backhands
breasts sprout from the canvas
a heavy impasto of imposters

in sunday best
dad's sermon
toiletpaper falsies
seed characters spit out
in shades of black & blue
the gaping holes thin fleshy
bone shadows
chopped
bored
stroked
coked & slaughtered
on apehangers
taken for a ride
with a daughter
on a sissybar
welded to her nipples

THE AWFUL NEWS
For Glen

trickles in
"Karen's gone"
we lost another one t'the road

dream vapors
thin willowy long hair
thoughts of her wet the eye
cold in the ground for New Year's
while the kid dreams the awful thing

X-mas morning a terrible phone call
like a punch in the mouth
the awful news
Karen's gone
it's a whiteout
terrible blues
hurtin' head t'shoes
at some point we lose
the right t'choose
the kid dreams
hearts surround him
on new years eve
don't worry Karen
he will always be among us
what's eternal is our sharing

LEIFO POEM
for Leif LaMela

can you see him wandering
uphill in a lil stetson &
pointy cowboy boots
can you see him running
with 7 guns under his arm
he stops to blow away a tourist
in his blue s.w.a.t. helmet
cuffs on his belt
assisted by puppy louis
browneyed spittin image
peanutbutter cookiemad
trailing a howling bloodhound
everybody knows the boy
ya seen him around
with one of twenty fathers
& mother a plenty
can ya see him wandering
your own dirt road
sleeping out a poker game
browneyed pointy toed
quickdraw starsky & hutch
microfantasy fertilized
with a ride in the bronco
or a day digging a leechfield
with dave & tommy
he got the badseed torn from his foot
laid back in pediatrics doin tv & toys
stackfull of comics
from the chicago boys
flatbed truck & the luck
to have his gramma sitting there
beside him   just a bit laid up

telling us to smuggle oreos
while his foot drains
the reservoir of us his family
while little leif sleeps
it's a good night to dig deep
and realize the luck goin round
what comes round & round the hat
circles & bills erode
as we rap in potent codes
"got anything to offer- auction
                read,   sing-"
for we gonna make a little stew
of love & money & mutual juice
can ya see him wandering
eating cookies on crutches
repairing back home again
trailed by puppy louis
browneyed quickdraw microfantasy
                fertilized
gonna get our boy back
with incredible hospital stories
ol starsky telling some turkey
how he got in a gunfight
defending hank the marshal
from some crazy cowboy

(A benefit for the Ward Kids Medical Fund - 1977)

NASTY CANASTA

shuffle up the hill
windsmashing silk & wool
the dealer sits in her kitchen
armed with ashtray and Cola
jazz dribble & bionic kid
january furnace bliss
blast of mumbo
mambo tongues flick
night tales
                    "pins & needles"
toes torn & bleeding
unveiled family closets
grandpa's shack
gramma'a houseboat
pine barons & closetfull
of harem delights
rapping   rapping
"three of a kind
laying together"
lieutenants of light
charlie parker hocking horn
for china white...
morrocan gnouwa
pipes of Pan
the pain of drumskins
the visitors with frozen pipes
the night no one comes
the dealer sits shuffling time
chinked tite open space
winter is a breeze

NALENES BIRTHDAY POEM   6/78

she's a Philly gypsy
with a butt like a national park
she's juggling baby & burgers
& a history of pizza sauce
she's spunky punk bumping
t'james brown juke sooth
she's darkeyed open mind peaking
off the great mama mountain tits
          & when she walks   her hankie talks
& her secret sauce
makes a nice slice
feel like a good piece
               & when she's dancing
the world feels right
cause she's done the rope-a-dope with love
been down for a count in the cities
had a baby on the mountain
she's steaming creaming & screaming
for "more — more
turn it up
make this bike go faster!"
faster-deeper-harder
downshift the velvet
satin skin
embroidered by a blue rose
          & when she walks   her hanky talks
yep! chuck berry's lil' kid sister
her nationality a scarf
she's cooking gypsy disco buns

feeding the masses
fielding the passes
that gets us across the hungry places
the saloon girl living next door to the minister
the classic frontier story
pure gold in leather & lace
the blue rose secrets
in a church full of skin flicks
   & when she walks her hanky talks
yep! chuck berry's lil' kid sister
butt juggling satin skin
nighteyed secret sauce
steaming creaming juke hungry
satisfying sister nalene
blistering the winter blues away
yep chuck berry's lil' kid sister
born in dancing shoes
makes a nice slice feel like a good piece
the classic frontier story
saloongirl feeding the masses
the blue rose secret shakin t'
"gimme some skin" & "take me to the next phase"

A WHITE FULL OF WHEAT
for Bert May

big yellow hertz tractor
shaking warm up
going home going home
bert alert hauling
60,000 lbs of contaminated
wheat off t'Oakland
to make white bread
trucks circlejerk the grain elevators
down t'san jose to get yogurt
& up t'chico to get juiced
70,000 lbs worth
driving a white
dropping a white
up up 16 hours a day
he's driving
surviving cops & scheduled
breaking 55 with cb brotherhood
advertising the whereabouts of cops
uniform of shades & a cap
eating up broken white lines
been broke down in Idaho
finally a night on the coast
chinatown feast & kimonos
then back into the big white beast
road is a tapeworm
eating his hours
tangerine dusk lights first snow high desert
high on the white
million cows await slaughter in nowhere nevada

we're roaring trying to make time
with twin diesel freight train
freight train hauling 82 cars
roadside rabbit contemplates asphalt suicide
big peterbuilts hauling ass
in the opposite direction
carrying america's needs
toys foods & plutonium
nightride annointed by blue running lights
drivers are divers into the murky
sleeze of truckstops
no overtime
the ramps are vamps treating the truckers like johns
3dollar hankerchiefs
10dollar shades
20dollar vests
it's Little America
26.50 a room
we sleep in shaking cab instead
100 trucks parked barking dizel breath
hiss & squeel of brakes
1/2dozen fat waitresses shoving coffee at me
"but i don't want coffee"
she musta found a special on eyeshadow
flirting with bleary eyed truckers
hardcore wyoming saddletramps
driving high with financial insomnia
white on top of white
the moon's up on the snow
bert jumps from bag
eggs & fries
he's heading towards cheyenne

he's on the CB
hey ya hey ya
looking pretty clean here
no smokey ya ya ya ya
ball it
the great sage nothing
but snow serape railroad scar
& oil wells pumping
rt80 sandstone mushrooms
& snow fences
microphone t'mouth
"hey guy hey guy
over the shoulder
green t'fort collins
green light t'laramie
speeding white on white speeding
home again the mountains
of miles the 70,000lbs juicing
homeward into boulder & unload
climb down off the whites
unload slow down slow down
snowdown firewood wife & kids

DANCING ON THE FIRE ESCAPE

for Dan Swenson

                    pine splits and the crowd sighs
              he works out the knots for kicks
to clear the air   kata trance
              imaginary bones splinter
body sags against the bodybag   for endless hours
bap bap whew whew   10 years   beating the mirror
consoling showers & plastic trophies
to destroy the vampires ignorance & awareness
he gets low   kicks back another border   refuses a limit
sweeps and destroys who he usta be
rings a cup   feeds back a club   tatoo's a face with a backfist
plays ribs like a piano   grins gracefully
into the eyes of his teacher
paying tribute to his mother
he's going for it now
charmed by his lover
framed by his students
a still life explodes
like some samurai mountain biography
he comes down off the mountain
to gush forth a fountain of gladness
"like the sun at midday"
furiously igniting the body as
a condemned building of habits
he climbed colored belts
now scampers on black belt fire escape
a second dan   attacked the impossible
& huddled the night with friends
sitting low to the floor
toasting each other in a mountain inn
laughing at battles
                          before he fades
like some watercolor samurai
back into the pines
on a cold nite in paradise......

FLOWER ARRANGEMENT OF COMPROMISES
MUTATES TO AMAZON POT PLANT

attitude of hardcore benevolence
memories re-run honeymoon
wrinkled, rusted & unable
to stand up to the rain
of everyday wear & tear
the little erosions of the soul
got so i felt like a silk print
kimono folded & sore
from absence...
deceides to either kill the kids or berzerk
changes name from rosemary
to ROXY... hardcore roxy
begins to trash her memories
go from a usual ivory bun & glasses
to flower arrangement of compromises
slaughtered with axe of radio music
husbands stash kids feathers &
warpaint, actually looking long slim
hair strewn appalacian Roxy- rocking out
kids walk in from school
husband home for lunch
radio on - sink of dishes
in lipstick the mirror says
bye kids
bye jo
      love Roxy
only thing gone is his pack
his stash   few clothes
the rent money
neighbors say she was last
seen hitching off in her kimono

POINTS & PLUGS

       the mechanic dutifully swears & curses
the malignant parts at the end of the day
she gets up on tip toes after washing the grease off her face
her hands crawl into his pockets
his rocket readies for takeoff
it's closing time she's opened him up up
up it goes she says "yep"
the boy's got something to disturb in here
verb in hair
the radio blasting sunset tokes
the lil' smokes the jets make over the divide
the bluechair hatching nightegg
change into streetwear cursing & swearing
wet toothy promises to go roam
get in the chevy get a beer & come
back to the garage for a rehersal
reversal of hours in monoxide & neon
sometimes i hold a hostage
mad enuf to eat his corpse on TV news
i watch them ring the building
tear-gas will be next
right after the reporters leave
i'm already an injured balloon
      he thinks,-
better get some of those fancy
rubbers for mary
on the way home
a ping & a knock invite
punches in the eye from timeclocks
timelocks   timelicks
so much purrrrr hour

cat's outta the bag
chase pussy long enuf
& pussy scratches you off the face of the earth
something smells fishy here
sardine remained the easy sucker of the sea
the high tide of your thighs
finally gives head to the stench
of crabtracks lowtide easyglide
'cross lil pools of your pride dyed in sunset bumsets
those easy upsets in the lifeboat you stole
back to points & plugs
those lil thugs of everyday
in comes sandman slowing down time
he rolls a fat one &
big brown heavy flowers
bloom for her birthday......

Totem

travelling
               elf peddling
up the trail of mad parrot

he crouches with his spear
listens to his fears echo back
listens to the demon in his heart
listen to his brain melt sanskrit
moves on
             travelling elf moves on
peddling his myth of nobody

Prison Letter From Johnny T'Bonnie

"hi, it's winter
the doc says
i have
cancer of the tongue
advanced stage-
they wanna cut it out
i'd rather die
than not talk
inside-
bye doll
write soon
you are all
i have."

WITH THE COMPASS SET ON
HIS GRANDMOTHER'S HEART

we were cruising down lefthand
xmas traffic thruway jive
last hugs
he's heading t'italy
heading t'florida
gonna smell the new crop
gonna smoke the no return
a cop a kid a deputy poet herbman
cruising across the plains
out come the baggies
fule up shovelling the winter snow
up noses up up up up up gotta drive stay up
talk up about out things all night
tapeplayer am/fm lies gossip hips of concrete
bank the curves smooth same ol 55 dont push it just
stay up coffee coffee drop in a lil coke up up up
writing poems & erasing them with more coffee
change drivers slurp more coffee eggs eggs
yeah more coffee please yes more eggs
truckstop nowhere dawn in kansas
trucks trucks pink streaks orange ya   morning coffee
up ya it feels good i been up all night up all night
driving the lil peugeot driving driving
morning mick up hungry & playing singing rock songs to
imaginary girlfriend herbman rolling fat ones taking the edge
off taking off after more breakfast & coffee pee & peterbilts
pulling out belching diesel all day in shades making raids in
the freebox coming at ya broken lines
& silhouettes of churches warehouses houses snowy fields
snowyfields endless cups o'coffee endless lungfulls endless
indianapolis chinese noodles nosing around at 55 55 55 is
the way no stops just keep going
with the compass set on his grandmothers heart

bowlfulls of pasta
gonna set him down
      end the binge of white lines
      as the road stops in front of his house
      as a butterscotch pontiac bubble skirts
& whip antennae 4 black brothers
      wave a joint t'us
      white willing & wasted
      on a thousand lil white lines
      -she's kissing an singing italian
      hugging micky shoving us down to
      plates full of peppers & eggs
      & nice clean beds begging
      slowing down long enough to'get up
      again

Dating Service For Four

i don't really wanna go
get my napkin squeezed
for a juicy story

the host looked so much
instant tragedy
there were four chairs
and three of us
what else could we
talk about

"SOMETIMES JUST UP THE HILL IS PAST POSSIBLE"

bowl cleanings & a bad temper
erased with clean hair
& the decision to go out
& do it
pick one up
& do it for money

on the corner
in the doorway
in the bar
looking cool
acting hot
thinking 'bout-
> wet snows dripping off
> Burnt mountain
> Kimono mountain
> the snowdrift on her coldframe
> your taillights
> at the end of the bed-
> so little gets said so fast
> but it won't last
> much longer than the money-
> i run mountain honeys
> thru my mind
> layin' for the 8-ball
> in a hustlers bar
> all day this phrase
> calling me
> "sometimes just up the hill
> is past possible"
> now that's where you'd go
> if ya was hungry in the mountains
> but Marroccos
> but this is serloin serious
> suckershots

meet a muse with a cleft lip
eat a clue
swallow the economic system
standing on the corner
trying t'remember who i'm to be
for bucks like- BONNIE BREMSER
BONNIE BREMSER
i dream of giving you envelopes of money
for all the times we've tricked together
laying back naked in a hotel called "the End"-
bonnie bremser bonnie bremser
is who i'd be at 33
vodka & soda & lemon
just melting in the glass
letting the johns in like sunshine
on a garden of money
of course, we'd only do it
when we're broke or sick
of coasting in neutral
or maybe in a bad period
seeds & stems
when you need the kiss of silk-
go milk a johnny cum lately

Statue Head Topples In A Cold Rain

sheets of water cold   curtains
window boxes
eyes crossed   the statue
leaned to death

                        with the throat slit
                        deep red gash
                        with nothing coming out
period   8 days late
period
          cold
          storm fallings
          build up behind a dam
the winds came
& turned the aspens black
gardens crippled
& the wildflowers walked with canes
the winds came
bringing high pressure zones
shelving thunderheads
& a spray of snow
the winds came
breath on the thighs
rock melt
snow belt
run liquid rivulets
of soft curly
waters lapping
gulch thighs
dewy grass
head buried deep
ruby eye
snaking
you came
q u i e t
lil' quiver
slight blush

light in the eyes
hairswoony
the winds died down
taut linen got
stretchers talking
bout the balance
of living on the divide
while my head blows off
you hold my tea cup
the weight of my hair
is evidence
my neck wound
demands a weapon
your pointed paintbrush
& silk dustcovers
listen to a will get read

MY NOBODY HOME

cigarette lighter
my sleeve's on fire

a throatfull of needles
sitting on hummingbirds

spiderturds
& blood custard

eyes of mustard
mute scream

rat silo
& generals

dreams of
my nobody home

split shakes
leaky poison

pose a guillotine
basket balls

sprout pubic
horror

garlic ants
crawl

nightfear
sudden fall

off a building
not   there

red splash
anyway

no
picnic

no
body

coffin &
tablecloth

entwine
death reclines

with open mouth
lulabyby

here briefly &
gone on the tide

clock keeps ticking
but nobody home

STOP THE WAR ON THE INFANTS OF COLORADO

the american spine runs north to south as rocky mountains
rising 14 thousand feet off a high plain full o'cattle & oil
the air is fine   the rock & snow last all year   its where you
mr & mrs america, take your kids in the summer-its also the
home of the ultimate bummer brewing down below in that
huge fenced-off area
with the 1100 security guards & their families & the families
of all the patriotic physi-fissionists live it's where the eagle
gets its trigger its mama was born in hiroshima daddy in
nagasaki its an area of beautiful meandering streams
finally reaching the plains before being sucked into
rocky flats nuclear bomb plant
It's a quiet deadly war on the white cells
of kids living in Broomfield & Arvada   just south of suicide
it's where the mutant workers live
where white cells multiply & die
multiply & die   quietly wither instead of grow
fission takes place in the marrow
cause the baby got thirsty
& mama turned on the tap for water
& out comes nuclear puke
into babybottles   in broomfield & arvada
poisoned workers drink cancer-water drive home in hot cars
full of glowing groceries nazi amerikan technicians
& nazi amerikan security guards
doin it for the money
close their eyes on their own kids
close their eyes to fields of deformed deer around the plant
sick jackrabbits   sick sick sick babies as bad statistics
don't it make ya jumpy   don't it feel so awful bad
not a cloud in the sky
not a blooming mushroom on the sick earth
& in that huge building over there
they make the hydrogen triggers

the technoniggers doin it for money
in the name of nat'l security
filling babybottles with leukemia for the sake of the country
right next to denver   to deter the russians
but ya know that jimmy carters kids
ain't drinking them streams
the war on infants in broomfield more subtle than nagasaki
but exploding kids chances the nazi amerikan naturewar
to multiply & die like sick jackrabbits
turn up the microphones   attack hearts thru ears
WORKERS STOP stop entering stop creating horror
for 2,000,000 years stop pulling triggers on the future
                stop   no neutrons   stop being atomic
cops stop the war on broomfield & arvada
stop filling babybottles with death death death
stop seeding the clouds with cancerous rains
close down rocky flats   stop the trains in their tracks
cover it in lead   make the powerfreaks atone
stop atomic junk tie off the tracks bringing in poison
to destroy the west with atomic meningitis
denver was written off as an experiment in urban anxiety
anxiety triggered by just turning on the faucet
stop at nothing to stop it   before it's all nothing
but deformed kids nourished on nuclear puke
                              nuclear puke
                              nuclear puke

FACT OR FRICTION

"Hey, Sugar"
big wet saturday snow splot
goes the sun   it was black
belts birthday & 1/2 of the
women in town were bleeding
or wished that they were
dogshit & a new judge were
both breeding contempt for
the bastard thet retired Eli the dog
into the dumpster.....
"we laughed alot -
we hugged & kissed -
it was spring and the town's
panties were sopping."
and so a few more bellies
burst with future voters,
after they are 32 days old
of course - - -
boredom got horny and rolled
a fat one - - - "off to see the lizzard
" she sang to aspen buds -
sunbathing in spring gulch,
 the bag of muriel's cookies
disappeared, suckin on a piece
of rawhide she hid from cigarettes
Oral Jones had just hit town
from another trip to the coast
with his own personal police
department, in l.a. leather drag
and the confidence that cums from
knowing the feel of custom rubber
grips erect in a pancake on the hip -
hip . . . she always wanted to make
law an order and planned her

110

ambush at the penny poker game,
he was never the same - - -
"Oral" he yelled - "more boo . . .more boo
how come nobody is scared of me?"
"chalk your stick man, & put
that thing away, ain't gunna
need it at this bar, tho
the women have your name
with gunsize and phone# - - -"
- she wrote it in her boyfriends
blood - which is why she was in
there for so long anyway -
her quarter was up
she racked 'em for tall bob
while he played with the cue
the 2, 5, & 7 on the break
he put his knees together and
ran the table - - - she hung up
her stick & sat at the bar, she
smiled at free drinks all night
she was workin out their kinks
by being straight with them
down the hatch
kinda givin head to their wallets - - -
everybody wanted it
but only a few actually got wet
into bed with some one
beside the usual snore -
the end of another winter
out, out, out!
he fired his black powder off his dirt bike
 an lit his darlings joint -
the days are cooking and nighttimes
the town breathes a little harder -
harder, faster, deeper, she
kneads sweet batter for sticky

buns - prepares another pot
of coffee & awaits another
onslaught of gossip - - -
another winter is over
jobs & grants do an indecent
exposure:
he whistles while he works but
all he can think about is jumarring
up her thighs as soon as the
avalanche danger passes - - -
the end of another winter -
less clothes an more kicks
outt'a home grown & mud lake . . .

Oh You

transient
sentient
black robed butterfly
with a scrimshaw grin
"the grass of oblivion"
letting go
quote Lao Tse
on killing flys
while shovelling snow
up noses from which
beautiful red bats fly
dripping blood
participate is a helicopter
ya can hear it coming
pushing possibilities into veins
trying to find the mother load

POEM TO INVOKE THE GODS OF THE POST OFFICE   POEM TO CONJURE UP LOVE LETTERS FOR OUR CAGED BROTHER JAKE THE DANCER
JAKE THE DANCER

tonite he sits in lewisberg pennsylvania federal prison
but his spirit is arisen
we work out & gather to braid the possibilities
jake does a series of a hundred in a million push-ups...

he came to town carrying a wooden indian
told fuzzy right off he was an honest criminal
with a recommendation from superstars off the ten
most wanted list
                    he joined ours   quick
within 48 hours he was a womens legend
he was too big not to believe
he had big harley arms jake the dancer hells angel
sweet hero of the underground
he'd done his time in prison
but nothing touched his spirit
he's bigger than life too tall to hide
he settled in   became a wildflower in a wild summer
became a town body-god   got folks workin out
                    flashing his grin
then he committed the crime of going home to maine
& they threw him in the portland federal prison
said he stole a load of pot from the coast guard
                    can you imagine that...
they squeezed a guy that ran off at the mouth for immunity
& he SOLD jake- in jail he organized misfits into a volleyball
team
                    got people jogging
pushing down on the cold concrete floor   he pushed them
                    out like his momma's prayers
they say he dabbled in tankerloads

they say he fed our heros when they starved underground
they sentenced him to do a weary 10 in lewisberg

                    JAKE SAWYER
                    #441149
                    box 1000
            lewisberg, pennsylvania
                    17837

                            8 9 10 2000 three thousand
drops of sweat pushin off the prison floor
in a cage that could never be big enough
in a rage of righteousness that won't be silenced
jake the dancer hones the edge of his high
thinks about us as the lights go out
& the touch of a letter against his chest
is what feels best

                            til the sun comes out
                            & the weights come out
                            & the mail comes in

MOTHER IN NEED OF A WIFE

bareass sunsoaker
                    ...eases
by leaking blood
on the garden
of children fighting
in pigtails
                    pig
                            tales
told & retold
to the sound of breaking molds
no more zippered fate
safety pins
popping pillows a soap opera
a hope opera a tragic songfull
a dirty diaper
shitwork
piecework
no more regretable belly
nope...
            motherhood hits town
starts a bit of hugging
starts holding a few tired hands
starts visiting
starts kissing
starts rumors
that momma got herself
a wife
... two 3 year old women
demand to be taken seriously
as the wave of the future...
two 3 year old women cuddle in bed
both wearing silk panties
                            enough said

the wave of the future
already runs amuck
in spring gulch-
gushing glacier blood
the old meltings
non returnable
no refund
down the hatch-
"MAN OVERBOARD"
hit by that young wave
helplessly bobs
while a thousand pair of
ex-dishpan hands
                    wave goodbye
but show compassion
by fishing him out
after the hookers get
a nice slow even tan
he lives   to change
after he climbs
a rope of babyshit
        the mothers of
        the world
        would say
-"WELCOME ABOARD"-

fullmoon
doghowling
only light
on in town
palm to palm
thru circle
gossipstop
open eyes
as cast dice
full scorpio
in treetops
silhouette of
nobody urges
mint to creep
up spinaltree
which is the leg
of a thing
giving black milk
to feed
garlic ants
guarding the motherlode
in creamy-light
zazen
rooftop
dog echo

GRAY

rainy train yards of denver
AMtracking slow lullabye
of steel wheels rocking
"Visions Of Gerard"
from - smashed printer
inky dinky
steel caccoon
plans of angels
change with every breeze...
corn stubble flys by
hard to believe
only this morning
undoing the knots
in my kids hair
i hear myself
railroading
echo of porcelin
urinal

WHEN THE LIGHTS GO OUT
FOR A FEW SECONDS

the foot forces the groin to pull the lightswitch in the eyes
the bloody mouth never says "i'm sorry..."
the guts must be cast from some kind of poverty
& yet you must fight back
& don't miss too many shots
or eat it yourself
the little birdies of fear faceless floor kisser
nope! not for me
you are just cheesecake in a sweaty gym
knifehands annoint the time you have left
caress anything but fun & there goes sanity
serious wants ignite neon confessionals
where cheapshot artists wait in the bathroom
guns are cheap at half the price
lice explore those that ignore the whores
waiting for a taxi till tomorrow
with clear plastic shoes
& heels whereever ya look
look again
duck the jab & hook
hock the alibi
& punch out the cards   bid   bite the rubber indent
the enemy head
bought & paid for with buckets of sweat
push-ups on the broken glass
you were constantly looking into
a solid right broke the mirror
there was nothing dearer but darling
look three feet straight ahead
crouching & drooling brute breathings hiss & bark
& then yer rattler nut shot & sudden knee
found you stomping & slashing the exposed parts
till even the gurgling stopped
& it becomes deadly quiet
& yet birdies

Siesta Time In The Artist Abode

9 o'clock evening silver clouds
the pines go silhouette
hash fumes levitate the artist shack
dos y media (siesta time)
blue windowed voyeur
on the full moon
the town lights moth about
here & there infants sucking
& the balance of spring heat
throbbing out there lil' cabins
divide & multiply
love blows the milkweed seed
laidback as the pasque flowers
but inside feeling showered
with changes   rearranges the flow
be it whiskey or money or sex
be you cursed with all the syphillis of egypt
no matter how bad how down
what is the great remember?
is it name or formula
shoulder to lean on
someone to tee off on
someone to be raped by
just one more time?
no it is the great tit hanging
it is the lime milk of spring
is the bluebirth   the redhead
fog on the rag
it is the ankles of summer
but for some the weaning is over
half a bed haunts the night
the night has come
the moon lights the great divide

it is clear - the great remember is
we are all on the same side
an easy glide on hot breath thermals
the pines are gone now
moon's laying one on us
nightfire cool milky veil
for anything goes!
it's springtime in the mountains
& we are them snowfields
dripping down ol Niwots thighs
our mind hears a sigh, then a roar
dos y media living inside you
entering a can of geshia mandarin oranges

Recently Discovered Electronic Music Causes Ulcers

Cahill:

      the first to make electronic music
      almost a hundred years ago today
      piped it in thru the phone lines
      to homes and businesses like muzak
      but he went bankrupt when somehow
      he blew out eight thousand phones . . .

you have gone to work
part of the music
you drive your VW
blow smoke & park
after winding it out
thru taxi brakes squeeking

there is nothing
that can be made
which does not leak

even birds leak
constantly
all dead things leak

grass has been known to leak
cloaks & daggers
dikes really leak
& we all know how little
boys leak

stewed tomatoes are very wet
so is rain to a kid
crawling on a damp peeling porch
floor

      loud piano noises
      massage in a hurry too hard
quick fuck to appease when really
dreaming of that bone china
      they're giving away at the bank
but it was raining so hard today
& the baby was sneezing   "yes jack
- - of course i love it - -
whatd'ya mean i'm not even wet!"
"- - today i had the repairman
a bitchy kid - - a broken umbrella
& you never fixed the roof
- - there were pan on the floor everywhere
& you say i'm not even wet!"
      well i'm pissed
& not only that but the phone rang all day
& the radio broke & the repairman talked
on & on about his ulcers . . .

CAN YOU COME

the history of an urge an idea bred & fed with peruvian
blizzards & columbian lungs bursting with roadfever
heading to the coast..joints annointed the last of winter
weariness& the longing for wonderful strangers unfolding
as friends in the mountains mouth t'mouth rush of
eucheristic boo   yaaa
booooo   yaaaaa no no must be something different than
that   some easiness unwinding relaxed just us
            out went invitations
                    can ya come can ya come can ya come we dare
ya to
come get down with us   mouth t'mouth
                                    plane tickets
                                    motor problems
                                    gotta leave a show
                            leave a family
                        fight a night
                    dance alot
can ya come can ya come can ya come up here
can ya make it up this high
can ya handle our love of new faces
we don't need fame
we need flames
need it to get hot
snuggle up & pull out your best
no test   just usgetting close
lighting up the night   sharing the moon
the stars are just the real ones up above
the treelines shot up noses trying to sniff out the alchemy
brewing
in what is about to unwind
now we're all here time to end the dry spell

light up a fat one   stay warm   get close
we're all here   can ya come
but it does get nippy at night
get closer
we are all here can you come
the orgy of bards is about to begin again & again
can you come here we are
the history of an urge
not to be quiet
not to let the prisons sleep in concrete
not to accept but to make waves to transmit
from 9000 feet to nourish each other from the great granite
tits
to come together   just us
                              unwinding
                              on a beautiful night in paradise

                    Opening poem "Can You Come "
                    Poetry & Kick Boxing Fest
                    Ward, Colorado August 1979

Pavement Dweller Poems
& Ballistic Kisses lyrics
1980 - 1986

WHOSE MAMA IS THIS

whose mama is this
whose mama is this
whose mama is this
whose mama is this
she eats her luch
facing brick wall
down by the hamburger stand
rain has stopped & begging's been fine
whose mama is this
whose mama is this
why is this happening
old bags of crying rags
ahe sits on one
and fights with the other
this ain't ronald reagan's mother
uh uuuhhhhhhh
not your mama
sleeping in an alley
shitting over a sewer
getting older & older
she'll never get newer
feeling like a sewer
getting older & older
she'll never get newer
feeling like a sewer
she's sixty-five years old
and she smells like piss
whose mama is this
she's looking for a doorway
in the rain
the cops don't even check her out

she got nothing
just secret hiding places
and bags full of rags
whose mama is this
whose mama is this
your mama ever slept out on the street
how come?
dog food madonna
ya'all blow more on dope
than she'll have forever
ain't the truth ugly
it's too insane
not to feel her pain
whose mama is this
somebody gotta claim her
somebody gotta name her
whose mama is this
whose mama is this
mama mamamamammmmmmmmaaaaaaaa
whose mama whose mama whose mama
whose mama
this ain't ronald reagan's mama
not a BUSH mama
not a HAIG mama
not your mama
not my mama
whose mama whose mama
whose mama whose mama
is this?

BLACK & BROKE

she was black
she was broke
she was running down the alley
from a vice squad cop
shoving bucks in her bra
she was ditching her coke
she was running outta hope

 chorus
she was black she was broke
she was running outta hope
she was black broke running outta hope
she was black she was broke
she was running outta hope

was a bad joke Monday night
cop was chasing hard
he was lusting a bust
using bucks as bait
she dove in to a cab
he almost tore the door off
he was pointing his gun
what a way to make a living
how was she to know
it was a cop that she was blowing
just trying to pay the rent
just trying to pay the rent
just trying to pay the rent
just trying to pay the rent
trying to pay the rent
just trying to pay the rent
was a catfight in the cab
brought the other whores running
slamming handbags on the man

a punch a kick
a flash a spurt
a slice of life that pig
lay bleeding on the curb
the cab's dragging her down the
street by her dress
the cop falls out
bleeding from the head
he wasn't breathing right
he worked too hard tonight

his gun lay in the gutter
feeling all alone
but it just don't feel that sad
she was black & broke & bad
he was black & blue & red
a cop half dead
now that cop he sits sucking sirens
gets detectives in mercedes
& a wagon full of dogs
that whore escapes
toward a nice new dawn
reflecting bloodstained cement
she was black
she was broke
she was running outta hope

chorus
she was black she was broke
she was running outta hope
she was black broke running outta hope
she was black she was broke
she was running outta hope
she was running running running running
she running running running

she was running down the alley
from a vice squad cop
shoving bucks in her bra
she was ditching her coke
she was black broke running outta hope
she was black she was broke
she was running outta hope
black broke running outta hope
she was black she was broke
she was running outta hope
but it just don't feel that sads
he was black & broke & bad
he was black & blue & red
a cop half dead

TOUGH SHIT

i was walking down the bowery
on the way to your house
i walked by an alley
and a knife came out
i staggered up to your house
& i fell on the floor
you take me to the hospital
they say "Are you insured?"

it's tough shit you got stabbed
it's tough shit they don't care
it's tough shit you don't have any money
it's tough shit cause you ain't rich

this mexican guy is driving across the border
with his wife & kids
tells the border guard "My wife is feeling sick."
that guard says "Beat it spic you ain't no american
you don't pay no taxes
it's tough shit cause you ain't white
it's tough shit that you ain't rich"

you go out to a club on a Saturday night
go up to the doorman and say "my name is on the list".
he says "tough shit I can't find it."

it's tough shit you can't afford a ticket
it's tough shit cause you ain't rich

this spanish woman from avenue D
she calls the police station "officer ya gotta help me out

i just been raped" he says "ave D? you sure you didn't
invite that man upstairs? better go get your ass scraped"

it's tough shit such a bad neighborhood
it's tough shit cause you ain't rich

as a matter of fact you probably got no money
this is new york city got no pity
get a job slob

tough shit cause you ain't rich

DOMESTIC SERVANTS

it rains it rains it rains it rains
it rains it rains it rains
ocean gets deeper every day
rich get richer
poor almost get paid
tropical dreams they fade away
& it rains it rains it rains it rains

domestic servants domestic servants
demand a decent burial

and the music in your head
the music in yo head
demands a decent airial

ocean gets deeper every day
rich get richer
poor almost get paid
tropical dreams they fade away
& it rains it rains it rains it rains

when you're dead it's immaterial
to demand a decent burial
& it rains it rains it rains it rains

ocean gets deeper every day
rich get richer
poor almost get paid
tropical dreams they fade away
& it rains it rains it rains it rains

it rains
it rains it rains it rains
it rains
it rains it rains it rains it rains

WATERBALL SATELLITE

These lonely frozen rivers
Dawns that won't forgive us
Make crossing over easy
On temporary terms
We saw it all before
Coming through swinging doors

Frozen rivers
      Lonely frozen rivers

Nervous rush for meaning
Taxi cab day-dreaming
Waterball satellite
      Lonely frozen river

These lonely
      Only lonely only lonely

These lonely frozen rivers
Dawns that won't forgive us
Keeping ghosts as pets
Place your bets – place your bets
Waterball satellite

EUROPEAN ASHES

They came through Germany at night
Got froze in their tracks by a tactical
Beginning of the end was practical

Leaders stashed
It was all planned
Issues not tissues
No one had a chance
        Then came the final sin
        With a cruise missle
        They took out Berlin
        Then they traded
        Poland for Holland
        Peking for Swedan
        Dublin for Chad
London turned to sand
Tactical strategic
Tactical strategic

A big one fell short
Took out the Pacific
No longer specific
Italy went neutron
Sculptures lived
People died People died

They came through Germany at night
Got froze in their tracks by a tactical
Beginning of the end was practical
Submarines waited off the coast of France
        No one had a chance
        No one No one No one
No one had a chance

ALPHABET TOWN

Ain't no future on Clinton St.
Needles are dirty & the dope is beat

Red tape black tape
Can't escape economic rape
Red tape black tape
Can't escape economic rape

Sleepy whores on Christy St.
Junkie boys in way too deep
Rats sharpening needles
Stainless steel mosquito's

Red tape black tape
Can't escape economic rape
Who ya kidding
Just tryin t' earn a living

White kids sell it for sport
That Spanish kid sells it for pay
Fashion boy goes uptown to wear it
Poor kid, he gotta stay

Down for the count
Never heard the bell
Fighting to get out
Punctured Arms Hotel

Red tape black tape
Can't escape economic rape
Who ya kidding
Just tryin t' earn a living
Sellin' spliffs & itchey whiff
Fallin' off them sidewalk cliffs

Nasty rumor
Said he had a social tumor
Buried him in brand new Puma's
Red tape black tape
Can't escape economic rape

Little tykes sellin' spikes
Off stolen bikes

Ain't no future on Clinton St.
Needles are dirty &
Dope is beat

"Yo – You talkin to me?"
"Excuse me, which way to Clinton muse?"
"Go on – get outta here"
"Betchya got a nice sister"
"I'd like a large bag of that black tape"
"Beat it BEAT IT!"

THE HEART OF ART

a poem to go a take out poem/nourishing the needs
to be shaken by art A R T prepunk wordthing a r t
the real raw   the stuff that smelled like clams
digging a saxophone on the rag
blowing some smoke outside a club
hanging out with each other is an art
instead of hanging just on walls
art as a newborn NuYoRican
in grenwich village stomping grounds
coffee grounds espresso fast walking
collar up trying t'beat the cold
leather coat art the punkychic thing t'do
in soho warehouse galleries
from slum t'slime
kohl beind shades theater dance
feels alive undress an address book
corner phone boots like some peepshow
walking the streets
art as hankies from backpockets
reading each other
like van goghs ear
hankies & keys & leather the flags
red fist yellow showers blue bottomboy
spreading his myth
just walking down christopher
getting read like a newspaper want ad
but nobody lookin In the galleries at night
instead its art in the dark
in the back of trucks
finger painting love on leather
art is everywhere
except in your paycheck
I found art   at the end of a shovel
clearing old asbestos to make the basement nice
for some artist to pay a thousand a month
art the poor thing
the rich got their claws into it

if you are collectable   they buy you
they always buy the latest rage
& so came punk puking on art
spit spikey & rude
singing anarchy in the UK
that is till they signed
&molested by their agent
while down on the bowry
below the biggest flophouse
the udeadboys writhe & drone
& the speakers bounce the bums upstairs in bed
nope art means nothing here
bowry a border for art that's been framed
prison walls another border
slums a border
                        who needs art anyway?
i do!
artists are creatures married
at too young an age to endless dreams
a high price t'pay t'invade yerself
& record it
work sleep feed the cat roll another one
gotta be more t'life than that
make art
the intangible come true/make things happen blush bitch
burst
colors changes rearranges
derange derange
look at all these arts
full of dope & hope
getting rid of despair
no more spare tireds hanging round
spend yer life scribbeling down
mindgossip in lil notebooks on 7th ave
artists sobering up on omlettes & coffee latenite
full of thoughts notebooking thru the streets
between the sheets
touching your typewriter like a lover

putting down the smell. of sex with a stranger
or the color of a dripping newborn baby
or a mountain cop doing his job as art
with a 45 & cuffs & mace & a joint to
cool out the near accidents he pulls outta snow
in his leather pants for him the heart of art
is framed in tite white slacks
saying "can i get you anything?
get me anything/spanish couples doing the hustle
nite after nite after a long day pushing racks
of clothes for the rich   they look into each others eyes
touch & spin t'program disco like latin maniquins
lil notebooks tucked in backpockets
feel like trapdoors to faraway cabins
ah yea pencilscars & sunsets as bums pets
art is too hungry to keep domesticated
gotta be masticated & spit out
reading the art news
american band from newyork the dictators
on their way to a gig in berlin
were picked up by german secret police
stripped in a rainy ditch
mistakenly as sympathizers of the bader mein hof
on the hoof pound for pound
art as sinsimillian buds
gone up in smoke
art will give you less & less
it's how the heart works
in & out in & out primal rhythms
new blood bathing tired cells
full of imitations irritations irrigating
media desert of blowing sands
art is in the eye
art is grass anchoring the heart
of art is full of complications
working out knots

art is always the young assassian
self portrait of rimbaud
walking across the alps
no ermine pussy   didn't need no nylon gear
just set out to go somewhere
write a poem scream In the wind cream of the moon
pound for pound useless & around since cavemen
got freaked by their own shadows the artist
gets tempted & tempered by the financial humility
of a rich society
trying t'finish a book paint yer heart out
pay the rent hold a job doing tastefull porn
bleary eyed on white crosses in some ad agency
painting   tiny mosaics
                persian miniatures
                ming dynasty
                noveau deco,
                expressionist exihibitionist
or nasty   new wave the heart of art
is making love
&your eyes
are the nipples of the revolution

FEELING LIKE A CASE

of all night doughnuts
lit by neon bare bulb
feeding pastry t'sculls
i frost the dawn
with lip prints pursued
late possibilities perish
& jukebox pouts1
last call
wishing for
just one thin thousand t'spend
& a spanish girl t'malke amends
but settle for making ends meet

when you took off your clothes
it was obvious the doctor
shot you full of low grade stuff
the cat flunked anatomy bad
your dream ended up
a bad example in a medical textbook

smoke a J
looked & got shook
made smalltalk
before i booked
going back t'the Lyle Hotel
shack up with a paperback

LAST TRICK EVER

old before, their time
victim of dye & make-up
& a bad case of the mirror
but once more
    slow walk
    sly glance
        dime in a pocket
eyes like heat seeking rockets
    hit a tourist from Montreal
        french horn player
          shy   but big bills
  & a garden of charge cards
        oh why not
    standing there anyway
  right in front of a window
full of fall wools & cashmere
  & this his third trip
  around the block
  around the block
  oh why not
        "last call"
  & she was a rentaholic
  but some tricks just don't wanna stop
  start smelling sweaty snakes
  wanna spend the night
  but not the bucks
  "fuck"
    reached in the hat
  to pull out a rabbit
  & realized she had a habit

The Guy Who Couldn't Tell
The Handle From The Pump

murray the man rolling up ounce after ounce
of missouri mule
& walking the streets
we would bet on whether the women
were real   or not-
look at the adams apple - look at the size
of them hands
"but look at the tits & the lips   the longhair
the walk-
i said "don't care man, she got a handle
jesusssss - ain't fair - looks good enuf
t'eat -
but would be just awful
like biting deep into a chocolate cake
& ending up with a mouthful of raw hamburger

"Hey You Country Boy"

where ya going?
oops just another clone
from the med center
trying t'fool a sucker

enough t'make ya
doubt yer own mother

can ya lend me some money?
front me an ounce
        just till tomorrow

            wanna have some fun?
            how much you wanna spend?
            hey you country boy
            where ya going?

THINKING

about friends in jail
everywhere i see bars
friends like used cars
with flats & tickets

jake the dancer
chuck & gary
helen & Jim
where do i begin
to
let you in
on the outs

cell blocks
ticket takers
cheap thrills
in movie stalls
on stagnant street

telephoto funnies
enough t'make ya cry
thinking about friends in
jail & me hanging out in bars

THE SAGA OF SALVADOR AGRON

it was the 50s & teenage warlords ran wasted thru the
streets seeking scars young savages in subways on
streetcorners luncheonets & pizza stands -didn't matter
where the blood fell
 it was blacks vs puerto ricans vs chinese & whites
 italian vs irish & the streets rang with zip guns &
switchblades
 as warlords in shades swaggered toward each other
as audiences applauded West side story

flash zip zip slash kill kill
nightfight run man run
but he was wounded fell
that terrible kid
did the crime & ate the time

15 years later
no longer a warlord
"resocialized & rehabilitated
sal skated toward freedom
on such thin ice
the governor gave him clemency
at xmas
springtime now in minimum security joint
no longer huge walls but
uniforms & a fence
he went to college every day
sociology & english
on a beautiful campus
in sight of the mountains
            touching trees
            almost free from 9-5
                but
                nights

nights he was locked up
no college kid
to the guards he was
just another spic
nope these good ol' boys
weren't gonna make it easy on him
why give a spic a break
instead of bars. . .
put him in a steel room
put him on a steel bed
keeplock
stick it t' this spic

who am i
free in daylight
locked at night
study & get high
till the prison bus comes
till the sun goes dowm down
& takes him back to the kennel
remembering
capeman remembering
dagger plunge
deep into the heart of a gangfight
on an asphalt court
uptown in the 50s
blood dripping down the knife
judge said "boy it's death or life"
sal said "burn me mister
burn my mother
burn my sister"
the court shuddered
& gave him the chair
 cut his hair
  tatooed his life with stripes

at 16 waiting t' get fried
but legislated dice crapped
another fate
commuted to life   behind bars
he taught himself to read & read
& write sal was a poet grew into a man
sinuey catsmooth education
push-ups & poetry
nothing t' lose
why not another jail tatoo
but he started digging
toward the wall reading toward
the wall & after a solid 15 years
for xmas the governor gave him clemency
almost free but not quite yet
transferred him to a minimum
prison of paper & wire
let him out 9-5 to go to college
but these new guards
hadn't seen him grow
he was just another spic
getting off easy
they started testing him
put him in keeplock
give him. a steel bed
strip him
then give him a four day
fourlough in the city
a tease of street
a taste of family
back on the bus
back to his cell
keeplock again
reality changes with the bus
with the sundown locked up

he was wearing thin as that clemency degree
just stay in line Boy!
split that image
lecturing on gangs to social workers
one day sal didn't come back
sal was headlines gone gone gone
they were calling him capeman again
sal was hitching thru the night
& finally two weeks later
hungry tired & burnt
after hiding in the arizona desert
he asked a cop for directions
to the salvation army shelter
they put him on a bus
fed him to the computer
& met him on the other end
of nowhere again
in handcuffs
capeman in the headlines
busted trying t find a breadline
forced to meet a deadline
teased by the sunshine
sal's locked tite tonite

REVENGE OF PUNK RAPE
(to those who have spent years deflecting rude cruises)

bent birth
raw steak
blackeye peeing
  porny piano
        steamy shower
        limp nylons
                scene sets
                while her
                leather loins
                itch & sweat
she enters
        front table
         window sits
          with no underwear
            squirming slowly
              slightly uncomfortable
                drinking in the window
                of the Palms Café
she clocks only herself
under orders from herself
deadpan in pancake
                no bra
  but tucked tite
  against left tit
  small black pistol
  just waiting for
    another man to pick her up
        usual short wait
        he glides up saying
        "what's happening baby?
she says sweetly-

"i guess it's you – draws
& fires BLAM
between his legs . . .
            waitress calls a boy
            to clean up mess –
            boy cops wallet
while she reloads
checks makeup
crosses legs
bare skin squeeks
sipping her drink
discreetly squirming
 till the next punk
                    COMES LEAD

AFTER FLYING AT 57,000 FT. TO MEET AN ANGEL ON THE BOTTOM OF THE BOTTOM BOTTOM

i just come in from the mountains of colorado totally blue & the air such good dope to breath & now here i am walking up west 4th to visit Damita staying at patrick stimulators place the fumes blowing in from Passaic petrochemical plants burning holes in the whore's nylons, West4th & the bowry, framed by chinatown the mafia soho, & the slobs on the way t'the morgue. damita had a baby, just had to see it, been on my mind for months wondering how she looked pregnant & high. lots of rich people renting lofts with a nice view of bums puking t'death & looking like the fathers of the spiked kids standing in front of the bar, this newborn month & a day already a legend at max's.

no doorbell, knocking but forget it stereo, cab & voice behind me -"what, ya got a case here your honor?", its Bill Bourroughs going up to his place by coincidence where Damita & Anya are hanging out- so we're yelling up to let us in, Bill looking his usual impeccable self in a gray suit & soft oh the softest green tyrolean hat & topcoat over his arm

Anya is beautiful lil' bowry angel oblivious to anything but a nipple full of love. She is close enough to CBGBs to hit a deadboy with a diaper or toss them down below as pillows to the wino freezing to death in his own drooling liquids -
even angels need a sip now & then

SMOKING

a big fat african joint
from the greenhouse in the mountains
after a $1.40 spanish omelet in the Valley Cafe
with the Sunday Paper served by a hard lookin'
      17 yr old chinese waitress

what a sweet tableful of trouble
hungover   hangin' out
eyelids embroidered by the morning joint
knowing only coffee will help
janie reads the funnies
jerry jet the want ads
damita scratched her purple head
all the boys in leather
needing eggs on a rainy sunday
the dribbling punkbaby mouths
& more coffee   more coffee
before another chinatown trick
t'feed the baby her formula
& get a bag for mommy

ah yea   life never felt better
warm friends & new heart throbs
me & tall bob
smoking a big fat african joint
just lookin' out the window
at the Hilden Hotel #31
it's been raining
lots of gulls swirl
sit & talk
roll another one of mule
talk about back home
& watch the radiator
like a fireplace

mommy's on her back by now
the baby with a sitter
its almost time for supper
still 1/2 a joint smoking
as the rain lets up
we all got a bad case of empty pockets
but the view is free
& we still got a big roach from that african

while momma gets slaughtered
by a bad need indeed
pumping pussy in a fish market
knitting veins in scar tissue
baby the issue
in her heart it's the rainy season
& love as tough as toilet tissue

GUILTY TIPS DOWNTOWN
(for the stoplight windowwashers- Bowery & Houston)

tonight i would gladly pay you to leave me alone. you had
spilled milk on that purple cashmere sweater & frowning
'cause the girl with the blue hair stiffed you and the boss
let the other waitress off early, now we're all screwed just
waiting for coffee & holding hands with cigatetts so cold
modern waiting our turn to use the bathroom, take yer
time with the check and thanks for the extra challah.

legs McNeil said "no thanks i don't smoke i'm a beer
drinker - this place is boring" . . . "so judge whatya think
of the mudd club?"
people trying to remember if i'm somebody or not
she whispered " i got a screentest with john waters over
dinner . . . i can hardly say it out loud . . .besides i'm sick
of screwing for a place to stay.

the guy on the first floor in the restaurant supply says our
crap is leaking in his cellar and he can't take much more
even though he likes us . . . us australians looking to marry
americans they'll never sleep with except on paper.

"PRAVDA" what a great name for a club but not on the
guestlist & couldn't get in, i said "i know jim fourat . .i
tried the passwords "pink commie . . . opportunist trendy .
. .give yaall head . . .nope forget it let's go t'the mudd &
make out we're somebody

wildbill bowery working out with his steel cobra in a nice
black sheath & the holster for his sap sized down right by
the shoemaker chap. bill be ready to blast some mugger
across the sidewalk like a box of sugar.

feeling nice after holding hands with a bowl of Kiev vegetable soup, cool night with scrapfires burning on the corners . . . skinnystreetjoint & the notebook in my head . . . on houston seven black boys exploding on a drunk, jumpkick to the head then smashing a quart bottle into a frozen broken halo in the streetlight till stomping put an end to his jerky movements . . . attack attack smash a fist into this one they're out bumkickin' looking for someone to ignite . . . new wave stupid crosses houston refuses t'listen he's so cool in his topcoat with collar turned up till they start kicking him & a cab stops & saves his life . . . they walked 1/2 a block and waited behind a fence for anyone these boys had real patience for developing patients . . . cops came 1/2 hour later. next morning after telling red breakfast stories i walked out my door to catch this guy in marroon sneakers suckershot this other guy & he's yelling like a nut let out too early . . . we can't handle too many more budget cuts at bellvue on our book . . . soon it will snow & cover up the broken glass but piss stains will reveal where the men fell asleep under that last warm blanket & the shivering in breadlines will keep the wine circulating and the men are counting on good tips around the holiday when guilt rolls down the window with a handfull of change.

PEACOCKS PREDICAMENT

shiftless doorway postures
sift dancing tenement stereos
tite jackets
open throated
young penguins
gawk & cruise

the practice is a balance
a balance between
street & firewood
polk st - tinker st
christopher st - modoc st
back alley chinatown
left hand canyon - rte 1
the queens highway
is littered with hickory
maple ash walnut beech
birch butternut hemlock
hard as rockmaple the roads
climb high into
aspens fir spruce & pine/away
in the trees for the asphalt
jukejive nightalive heat throb
pine away in small hotels
for hummingbirds & eagles
for columbine for old depot faces
so sit
shooting tracers
wear a robe of eyes
that turns insides-out
to a geisha with a

fan of foodstamps
shooting tracers
eye t'eye
a door of bees
the endless miles
with chains of gossip
pulling switchblades on snowstorms
what a laugh!
           the shiftless
doorway postures
endless as the firewood
we'll need for the rest of our lives
christopher hickory heat throb
backalley queens highway
pine-away walnut geisha
shooting tracers in this
small hotel of eagles
littered with a robe of eyes...

An Angel Bestows His Blessing Upon Them
(A Wedding Poem)

When they looked upon their brother
 It was a time of pain and darkness
When they looked into each other Love ignited a spark of
glowing light

> Their love grew wings
> And sorrow was replaced with wonder

For God so loved the world
He gave Joe and Cindy to each
other
For all who believe in love
Will reap the Blessings of Angels
Love heals and surrenders
Only to truth and tenderness

> To have and to hold forever
> To care and to share forever
> This is their Guardian Angel's wish
> That we fill this day with laughter and joy
> For we believe in the love of Angels
> For we believe in the love of Angels
> For we believe in the love of Angels
> As our Angel believed in us.

MAY 6th 1995,
Waterbury, Ct.
Our Lady of Lourdes Church
For Joe & Cindy Varrone

Don't Fall Off The Mountain
1997 - 1998

Eternal Return

(for Muriel Lawrence)

asleep in your bed
it's finally warmer
smoking your pipe
it's finally calmer
listening to your cookbooks
talk about art
finally home again
with your ashes on the hillside
beneath a blanket of snow
after burying my dead
lifting crates for endless rent
finally home borrowing your bed
knowing mothers are forever
& never accepting never
a sly o'l fox
comes barking
& visits your fire

Indian Springs

sit & soak
boil with friends
cave full of steam
bubbling pools
full of each other
untie the knots
uncork the things
relax the springs
enough to let go
let go
the meat tender enough
to fall off the bone
soaking under ground
let go the frowns
relax the clench
waterfalls of sweat
soak stone benches
let go let go let go !

A Poem For The Survivors

Oh Carolyn!

there were no heroes
but joyous survivors
sprayed the adjacent pine
steaming house next door

floodlit smoke volcanically tattooed
the night sky nobody
mentioned the lack of wind
for fear of conjuring
a bad invitation;
no uninvited gusts

containing her embers
this sacred task
to suppress flames with hope
that l'il cabin survived other
disasters heroically now
billowing smoke
the tribe from Indian Peaks
put out a fire
& tended a friend

the site sits cleared
under a blanket of snow
spring thaw & blown seedwill find a home
to make amends as joyous
survivors walk by & sigh
"I'd like to think she's happy"
her books finally put away
& finally rid of her own ruins
with the wildflowers of June

A POEM FOR KINDRED SPIRITS ON AUSPICIOUS OCCASSIONS
(equinox 1998 at the request of the local heathens)

it is time to accept
with open arms & mirror mind
the great mother taking a bite
out of herself
like a piece of ripe seedy fruit
dripping wet reds & aspen yellow
bloods & browns -
the maiden comes laden
with seeds for the future
gather the feast of promises nurtured
rattle in your empty heart
seed shakers & gatherers grind mind
polish the bounty of sublime
let the burden of strawbosses
go up in flames   dig & pull
seperate the sheath from the head
of wheat of corn of promises
each kernal reborn -
"death is certain on a full belly"
the maiden comes laden
with seeds for the future
reaping the past
without raping the future
the season squats over our families
and deposits a lingering fog
aspens promise to renew
by finally putting their sacred gold
back into the ground -

listen to her
she creates she conceives
she destroys simultaneously
the end begins -
sustaining heritage for a fin
(price as nice)
she matures the cycle
of sex & fertility
wealth & prosperity
she rejects no one
she is teeth dripping
pomagranite seeds she
is grinding us into mush
dazzling colors dripping
down her thighs   she loves
mice running up her twigs
sunflowered eyes drooping pregnant
praying for a breeze
t'scatter mascara jays
she knows what is coming
it's all right diminished light
slow down
listen to the quiet riot
end of strife
summer thunder gone
rut begun elk bugle
creek gurgles before ice
the sound dying
the dying sound
of 800,000 korean coffins
full of bones
lowered to the ground
instead of seeds

the teeth of politics
with endless floods fertilizing death
a sacrifice harvest of human pain
on auspicious occassions
kindred spirits contemplating equinox
the maiden comes laden & overflowing
together the knowing
beneath the coming darkness
promises nurtered
to let go the old
and renew the new

Kisses Or Caskets

life is a battle
death has a rattle
come along now
listen t'the tat
tat tattle
it's too late
to elect a slate
too late to suspect
too late for rebate
too late for respect
we could'a worked it out
we didn't hav'ta shout
i never meant for it
to turn into a bout
didn't hav'ta be a rout
we didn't need clout
but it's too late now
to make amends
it's even too late for depends
we could'a worked it out
we could'a been friends
we could'a ignored a race
didn't hav'ta win or lose
could'a turned the other cheek
didn't hav'ta save face
but it's too late
because there you lay
too late t'pray
too late t'say
it's too late
it's not fate
it's just way too late
tat tat tattle
death has a rattle

come along now
life is a battle
Ma's gone Dad's gone
nephew gone gone
gone swinging gate
gone gone long gone
once gone forever gone
sorry I'm late
it's too late
to talk about oiling hinges
regret arguing binges
it's too late to recall
what the yelling was about
threatening bruises using laws
broadcasting each others flaws
there ought'a be a . . .
but it's too late
to date or share a meal
make a deal a cake
or a hug it's too late
yer growing a rug
it's just too late
unless we look on the other side of us
& smile for a mile
before we hav'ta look down
on that final frown
each other can discover
Life is a battle
Death has a rattle
come along now
listen t'the tat
tat tattle

DON'T   BUY   NIKE

Nike abuses it's workers
Viet wage slaves
Slapped by Korean Warlord
Nike Bosses
Women must beg for
bathroom pass
must beg for water —
assaulted with Nike rubber soles
about the head and shoulders —
These shoes are created in the blood
& sweat of Viet wage slaves- They get
$2.50 a day & you pay $150 a pair for
AIR DEATHS
Refuse to make eco-war on
Viet wage slaves
Refuse to insult yourself
by buying their ads
Refuse to walk in their footsteps
light this fuse
refuse refuse refuse

JUNE 30, 1997

172

Lightening Strikes Twice

and I continue my life
a fair days work chopping words
all day wandering among friends
i plant deep within the ears
things grow quickly in July
things t'do before i die
why ask why
i see nothing
a sty without an eye
laughing uphill thru red red
red paintbrushed red red
i am on a flower bender
and i continue my life
sitting on a stump
in paradise
          let it suffice
lightening strikes twice
and i continue my life
deep within the chopping
wandering in paradise
red red laughing uphill in July

The Trail T'Isabel Glacier

for Phil Dubitsky

this is the trail that changes t'snow
the further ya go - changes t'rock
changes t'ice - this trail that
changes t'cloud - where thunder is loud
this is the trail t'Isabel glacier
this is my mind eraser
this is the trail that nails the grail
this is the trail without a rail
this is the trail that always begins and never ends
it's 18 years later
the trail is no wider
a bit more trod and muddy - walkin' and talkin'
one looks down d'mound
stopping t'gape into paradise
walkin' through landscapes of survivalists
red snow - lichen bitten columbines
in melt holes - constantly one foot
in front of the other
on arrival - the eyes strain to behold
the great divide - the spine of comprehension
look up ! UP! - rocky broken teeth from
peak t' peak
rippin' off the prom dress of the goddess
cloud shredder in a tight blue sweater
on a daily basis - no stasis - nor staircases
just lungs smokin' - inhaling miracles
a sudden plunge!
I fell through the snow bridge - cold meltings -
boot suck - snow - walls fall into raging waters
'till a strong arm angels me
Phil reaches down and hauls me out
of a raging funnel - eternal tunnel t'spit out
Could'a sworn I heard the wing beats

now up, up! follow the others footsteps
up up into wind - raped, cloud kissed
wailing wall - 1000 feet of rock around
I'm calling my gone friend
my sisters melanoma slaughtered son
TONY! TONY! and you kid echo back and
I know it's time t'climb inside
the great divide - : left you up there
with a blanket of snow and everywhere t'go
while i settle for a dry suck and hugging my angel
intoxicated with Philly on the rocks
and memories of clouds
shredded by rocks
and an afternoon of shared rainbows
across the great divide
Hey Tony boy! soar galore and rest in peace
within the silence
would'a swore
I heard wing beats
this is the trail t'ourselves
this is the trail going right here
this is the trail t'each other
sisters and brothers keep moving!
ya can't buy it
can't own it there's no deed t'the sublime
this view is for you and you and
forever mine
and definately swell
walkin' with you
on the trail t'Isabel Glacier

MIND MOVES HANDS

she heaves   -

he pitches

she dumps   -   he looks

she lifts & looks heavy

his eyes sigh

they've laid it on the bottom

& now it's time t'see

if they   fit together

tite

lock it deep

-

he adjusts

-

she places it in the crack

Tommy and Carol are on the level

this has been a rock attack

t'shore up the past

rock after rock after rock after rock after rock

Tommy & Carol are on the level

Mike Parker 8/97

176

Firefight

Duff glowing off the Sourdough
downhill t'nowhere
following the need
to quench the fireseed
got lightening spit
glowing red & white smoke
in the night - the tribe
from Indian Peaks
waterpacks & pulaski's
follow their noses
after an hour of running
the fire down
                the fire down
helping it drown
spade muck a lasso
of steam! taking control
the tribe from Indian Peaks
going home on a windless night
fire's out - sleep tite

BEING CRUDE

we
are the biologic
weapons to stop
before it's too late
we invent
crude reasons
to destroy each other
we
are the biologic
weapons to stop -
we are the deepest
pools of crude
to pump dry
before more Iraqi kids
die we
are the biologic weapons
to stop
      being crude -

THE RITES OF SPRING
(THE RIOTS)
4-97

the creation of a vessel
able to hold
the emancipated versus the confiscated
the right to the creation of a vessel
bare arms & breasts & tests
the brains rain growin' spring
ah! the unrest the social tests
the myth retread
the will to bend like willows
for each other as pillows
to fill the fallow
with pleasure & leisure
& truth t' dare
the consequences
instead of fences
Ding Dong!! we all belong
pestle & vessel
a union working for
ordinary gods & goddesses
just - be - cause
spring brings warmth & wet
a removal of protecting garments
pretensions dropped
of chained males
get that bush burnin' babe!
things are exactly what they seem
the seeds of human kindness
da' kindness battling t' break free
seed spreaders & planters
pushing beneath the moist
creates a new choice
t'view the private parts
of the universe
let the mind go — huang po

like a handful of newborn bear
hear the wild kitties on our horizons
feel the push
of pussy willows
thru beaver dams-
now the hand that tills with care
leans against the tool &
that lingering stare replaces fear
with a maypole -
& share the giving
the for-giving
receiving the maypole
po- po'nuf t'chase a chicken

better than tryin' t'make amends meat
chicken chokin'
on slip knots
hand-me-downs
& feel me ups
just like the ol' daze
but the grazin' is the same
slim pickins versus forget-me-nots
t'work it out
we sure   are attached
t'that stringed thing
we're all hopin' t'make music on
(here I could do a commercial
for altar sponges & sacrificial plans
or   the bran in the myth was
the fools gift   his mouth t'
mouth rush of euchristic boo
YOO-HOO! get the mop!
enough of winter
enough of enough
enough of looking
up a horses hole
to anoint the dream with fertilizer

fermented in privacy
vented at meetings
which way did you go?
ah yeah the importance of riots
outta our minds
accidental meetings comin' around corners
might suffice t'break the ice
which melts the borders
of established order
& cold meltings boil
the plundered friendships flooding
common ground
soil in need of water
cold meltings boil -
off our self importance
tryin' t'pose as bored elves
& hairy freelance fairies
caught with hands in the afterbirth
of each others needs to discover
what's for supper!   that's rite
put your blessings where your mouth is
and chew before you choose
t'take miracles for granted
das a rite
listen to your heart
grind greatness
from the human mess
wandering in awe
like the tortoise
visiting herself
without knocking -
but here & there
oh! here
& there
in the high grasses kisses
kisses in the moist spots
t'quench the dry rot

kisses in the choice spots
stamens stabbing dew drops
wallow in the hollow
close your eyes
inhaling nose t'nose perfume
instead of go home alone cologne
kissin' lickity splits
splittin' goin down on alone
no more atoning
hear the inner tides moaning
cold meltings boil
in each other
taste the soil
let go the constant toil
touch the mossy wet
for a brief time
keeping each other as pets
a yen for yang
a yearning for yin
let the games end
& the dance begin   again
& again & again
listen t'the hissing steam
taste the rising cream
blow on the flame
& pass that torch you're carrying
for someone
burnin' up inside
the boiling tides
unbridled sighs
the rites of spring are
beyond asking why
cold meltings boil
we've broken the ice
cold meltings boil
cold meltings boil
cold meltings boil

A MODERN HISTORY OF CAMBODIA

Pol Pot is dead
bombs are made of men

she brings gifts of red
clay bowls full of blood

she is having her period
the other women coo her

she has sacrificed image
another woman shags her hair

oiled &
rubbed into a sleep

her silks are made ready
she will be bathed in milk

the fires roast a pig
drums fuck madly without cuming

a golden bowl of shit
is served to the victim

she will deceide if he
will lose his or not

bowls of silver wait
to catch his parts if

that is what she deceides
for bombs are made of men

& the world has begun again
no more planes

no more
classifications of hells

the bombs are thrown to remind
them

small silk bags are filled with roses
& parts of them

many thousands of little bags full
are tossed from convertibles

it goes on for days
til the populace loves them

there are no old people
left

their ashes turned white
& blew into nowhere

nowhere is
a bone t'kick

or make
music *with*

with is a word
to color it

white is so alone
ground thundering LBJ's bombs

b-52's scorched earth
& from these terrible ashes

agrarian terror; kemher rouge
were born t'slaughter culture

a teenage army
made eye-glasses a crime

thinking or blinking
punishable by murder

Pol Pot is dead
Pol Pot is dead

cotton balls proof
his silent nostrils

it snowed all day up here
plow scrapes the road clean

suppersmoke annoints
our foul weather

Pol Pot is dead
Pol Pot is dead

even piles of skulls
attempt a smile

HRYNYK Wandering In The Land Of The Handless

you were a hands person
who laughed milking music from ivory
& i was all mouth
with altitude attitude
& we hung our art on the bowery
making music that refused
to ignore what was outside-
this mornings mail
(from the land of the handless)
said it was the plague again
killing my friends
that didn't believe in sin
or sickness but did believe
in singing about our common mess
ah catch your breath m'friend
& I'll do my best to shout
memories into promises
& continue testing the best
intentions my brother
intentions
like wishing
i had another coin
for this peep show
all those nights in the mine shaft
joints pulled from sockets ecstatic
taking on all comers
hung from the rafters
press into anonymous memories
a smile like skid marks before disaster
then wandering home
dazed & demented he cemented
melodies with invective
he sighed & laughed
throwing his last coins from bowery window before sleep
dreaming from mindshaft to his musical attic
he left a trail of musical static
entering the land of the handless

greenhouse drips
cold meltings
spring snow waters
my cherry tomato
& those white radish
seeds suck snow
plop! & melt through
a hole like unified
theory just another
leaky outhouse -
gamboge dandelions
limp raspberry
my iris bows
t' spring weather

DAYS OF HATE

in Denver hate is on a bender
assassinating cops carving his name in a slain pig
waiting for the bus a black refugee dead
a single mother tries to protect
they skin her forever
with a bullet severed spinal chord
for an ideology adored by skinhate
skinheads triggerfinger ignorance
hate has a date at a bus stop
STOP   STOP   STOP
last stop lost causes terror tactics
fed by youth just cultural bait
tossed overboard for racist ultraright
always wrong
can'tbelongs acting tough in throngs
the hungry ghosts of hitler youth
beyond bald fashion
festers aryan feet
stomping out a black man's life
a mother's hope- Jeannie VanVelkinburg
would do it again- would you
next time you hear nigger or jew
Organize your love- Destroy race hate
remember please remember
that terrible week in Denver
when hate went on a bender

SHOULDERS
poem for a peace officer

How many fires?
How many false alarms?
How many skid marks?
How many dogs?
How many deaths?
How many domestics?
How many lost kids?
while we enjoy dinner
while we went back to sleep -
these are the shoulders
community is built on
a miner - a blaster -
a whisky-sippin' grandfather
taking on our disasters
radio in one hand
a soggy sandwich in the other
a bear bopper - fire chief - Marshall
taking on our needs
somehow always there
because he dared to care
because he dared to serve & share
when your hand's ripped open by a saw
        when your heart's broken from feuding
dealing with threats of shooting and looting
when you're after a lynching
a cinching   a cursing   a curing
from out of the background
a source of strength with compassion
without a ration
these are the shoulders
community is built on
solid   willing   &   able
setting underground earth moving records
with Big Randy and Jerry Wayne
his shoulders lifting firehouse walls
how often we are in his shadow

blasting nipple-headed idiots
& our own small wars
he's the dream of employers
yeah! the mine owner Norm Franks
dreamed of hiring a huge blond
Norse god to wield his hammers
and place his timbers
and he's telling the guys
his dream the next morning
as Norm climbs out of a car with Ed Warren
looking for work -
Muriel's first night in Ward
a mouse chased by a cat
runs down her sleeping bag
and upstairs half asleep
she can hear this huge man
softly laughing -
he cradled cancer in his arms
and destroyed our inner blazes
ah yeah!
How many fires?
How many false alarms?
Skid marks?
Deaths?
Domestic quarrels?
How many lost kids?
While we slept
These are the shoulders
community is built on
for the safety of our lives
for the friendship and family ties
we thank you Norm
now let's echo that thanks
close your ranks and raise your voice
for giving our community choice
Thank You Norm, Thank You

July 4, 1998

190

Kids Poem

when thunderstorms come
little kids run & run & run
home to mama for cookies & fun
Nolan & Charles
livin' in their woodsy bus
no need t'fuss
listen t'the rain
little guys won't rust
let the thunder Boom Boom
hear that ! smack ! smack smack ! !
hail bouncing off the roof
when thunderstorms come
l'il Nolan & Charles
run & run & run
home t'mama for cookies & fun
now run & run & run & run

spring menu

dark l'l spider
hiding in the first bloom
of a pasque flower's
afternoon spread

Deaf Trout

W'E went fishin' at Red Rocks Lake
Pulled out the sunscreen and started to bake
Doritos in one hand screamin' worms in the other
Hayden lookin' around for Emma his mother
Sperl fed him sandwiches
Pete 'n Cliff hooked their dreams
we tried flies, spoons 'n potato chip schemes
up to our ankles - in over our heads -
the louder we got the more trout went to bed
twenty-two kids
six tired adults
rode home from Red Rocks
one trout under their belt
Nolan & Charles - Cody & Jake
Cole & River - chased
Kiam & Eric around the lake
Mika & Kwana pulled slugs from their toes
Logan & Toby pulled bait from Pace's nose
all the other fishermen left
so did the trout
except the one that was deaf

July 7, 1998

Look Out From Your Homes

upon that ocean of clouds
above a sea o' pines
the other day
i was a squall
on the bay
tipping the skiff
& accusing the oars
muttering about "capitalist
givers"
shivers in July
waving ba-bye   ba-bye
here come high tide o' sighs
angry whitecaps muttering
just a squall on the bay

afternoon thunder

the front's fire
streakin thru town
sound down shaky
hysterical showers devour
downhill soil wild roses
& fireweed blowing a bow by
chipmonk mowing my salad greens
things are exactly what they seem
afternoon thunders
angry gray
busting off the great divide
rolling
toward Kansas with a warning
hysterical rain beating down
afternoon thunders past town

full moon

from my
chopping block
stares
yeah stairs!
i climb toward you
leapin' them in pairs
leaving care for
meteor showers
behind a dark cloud
moon takes a powder

First Sip First

become that thirst –
quenching handfull of water
before you've gone
                            gone
                                gone
that handfull of water
so briefly held
but so satisfying
to finally taste
before your relatives tears
there go all those years – gone!
become that thirst
better tasted than cursed
first sip first

Ethnic Cleansing in Fraser, Texas

three white men
graduated prison with a degree in hate
drag a black man to beyond
death behind their pickup
until his body falls apart -
this is ignorance choreographed
into the womb as tomb
three white men executed
him for being born
for walking home alone
now they'll live 'til they feel
the needle going in
for ethnic cleansing in Texas

Sweeping Out My Heart

kickstart my art
back home high again
no longer defending
the things I must water
every day; it sprouts
a play about a night
with my father desperately
trying to breathe through tubes
readouts ticking
tubes dripping
last sleep
our last words
now promises t' keep
in between
this digital intervention
that drains a man's history
thru clear tubes
measure him his liquids
through a sewer
& me by lack of sleep
they know not what I keep
I still dream of digital beeping
& him moaning to wake
wondering who'll take care of his wife
& who'll take care of his wife?...
how many brooms does it take
t' sweep these scars.

To an echo of wing beats

Nolan watched the wheels
go over him
but there was something
inbetween him and hurt
Below him was the dirt-
above, the bottom of a car
& in between
something for a second
between him and hurt
this six year old angel
went inside himself
he didn't scream
he listened
to an echo of wing beats

Fog Falling Over The Edge

Isabel glacier rock fall gossips
across her dirty face
fog falling
cold fingers
prowl my spine
not even my
is mine
snowblast
wind brawling whitecaps
september's pulled the plug
waiting in the shadows
of meteorological thugs
glazing glacier
mind eraser
can't hear myself
return t'cabin
over the edge!

The Clinging

there are creatures that endure
mountains of pain
without a complaint
without a refrain –
there are those who inspect it
reflect & protect it
like buzzards & crows
the moon knows
mt. Niwot shudders & strains
without a complaint without a refrain
wind screaming timberline
ancient cedar & spruce
stunted crushed distorted
crippled avalanched bent
dwarfed deformed & thawed
no weaklings or cowards allowed
intimate with clouds
winds screaming at them
but they refuse to give in
rooted in the want to be
they keep their secrets from men

Seasons Change

the creeks we follow
lead t'the peaks we share
we rearrange our insides
our moons moaning tides
allow the light t'hide
& rock from side t'side
let the truth sink in
times tinder ignites
your glad glands glowing
the creeks we follow
lead t'the peaks we share
the need t'care
to rearrange our insides
moaning tides
snowy peaks
our muddy trails
as destinations - fascinations
& reputations melt & freeze
our seasons change
truth sinks
& tenderness ignites
see by our own light
the creeks we follow
lead t'the peaks we share

caraway claws stalk the cold
blowing snow, testy winds
daisys kneel as whitecaps
gossip with Gold Lake
a pair of osprey swoop -
a trout says its last prayer
in the air,   my nephew
when i dwell on you
i hear wingbeats
not in retreat but soaring
like the wind off the Indian Peaks

Don't Fall Off The Mountain

especially at the end of your rope
grab onto hope
scope a new route
up your own weathered face
keep breathing
keep breathing   keep breathing
let the rest rest
begone the gossipy heart
and mind as pest
as real as it gets
this is not a test
i repeat
don't fall off the mountain
this is not a test

about the author:

Mike Parker was born in Waterbury, Connecticuit, a brass mill town in 1944 and was educated at The University of New Haven & The New School for Social Research.

He has performed his work in nightclubs, coffeehouses, libraries, bars, universities, book stores, rocky flats, state penitentiaries, county jails, radio, mtv, grammer schools and mountain tops. Mike resides at "Dos Y Media", the Artist in Residence cabin at 9250 feet above sea level in the town of Ward, Colorado on the edge of the Indian Peaks Wilderness Area